**Other Books in the Kaplan Higher Education Career Series**

Your Bright Future in Information Technology

Your Bright Future in Health Care

# Your Bright Future in Business Administration

By Marilyn Pincus

**Kaplan Higher Education**

Simon & Schuster

NEW YORK · LONDON · SINGAPORE · SYDNEY · TORONTO

Kaplan Publishing
Published by Simon & Schuster
1230 Avenue of the Americas
New York, NY 10020



For bulk sales to schools, colleges, and universities, please contact: Order Department, Simon and Schuster, 100 Front Street, Riverside, NJ 08075. Phone: (800) 223-2336. Fax: (800) 943-9831.

Kaplan® is a registered trademark of Kaplan, Inc.

Contributing Editors: Karen Baldeschwieler, Anthony Poet, Dick Dormuth
Editor: Eileen Mager
Cover Design: Cheung Tai
Production Editor: Maude Spekes
Interior Layout and Design: Hugh Haggerty
Desktop Publishing Manager: Michael Shevlin
Editorial Coordinator: Déa Alessandro
Executive Editor: Del Franz

Special thanks to Grace Freedson's Publishing Network, LLC.

Note: Dozens of websites have been mentioned in this book for your convenience. It is possible that these sites may contain inaccurate, outdated, or objectionable material. Please be aware that the author, editors, and publisher of this book cannot vouch for the accuracy or integrity of these sites or any information contained therein.

Manufactured in the United States of America
Published simultaneously in Canada

September 2002

10 9 8 7 6 5 4 3 2 1

ISBN: 0-7432-3062-0

# TABLE OF CONTENTS

# ABOUT THE AUTHOR

**Marilyn Pincus** has written for all the major publishers of business information. Based in Tucson, Arizona, she owns and operates Marilyn Pincus, Inc. She writes policies, procedures, and similar specialty material for corporate clients and foundations and ghostwrites nonfiction trade books for other authors. Her books spotlighting business success skills have been published in eight languages and are read by people in many countries.

# INTRODUCTION

## SETTING GOALS: 101

**Question:** What can I do with a degree in business administration?

**Answer:** Almost anything! After your initial schooling and training in entry-level positions, you can work your way up the career ladder to become an accountant, banker, store manager, public relations specialist, insurance executive, or financial planner… and this is just the short list!

Your definition for success is a personal one. Still, it's good to know that with this degree so many things are possible. You don't have to know exactly how you'll earn your living as you begin to work toward a business administration degree.

### Taking Charge of Your Future

*You* are in an enviable position. *You* are taking charge of making a decision that will impact your future happiness. Some people who are about to further their education don't take charge. For one reason or another, they simply drift into a career choice.

- Jim's dad is a bank president and his grandfather was a bank president. But Jim likes working with children. During the past three summers, he's worked as a camp counselor. During the school year, Jim helps coach his town's Little League baseball team. He thinks about being a teacher but knows his family expects him to pursue a career in banking.

- Beth and her neighbor Emily have been like sisters since they were little girls. Emily wants to be an accountant. Beth doesn't know what she wants to do, so she decides to take accounting courses with Emily, even though she's always hated math.

Maybe Jim will be happy as a banker and Beth will be happy as an accountant. Who knows? Our point is that it's possible for each of them to make a well-informed decision about the career that's right for them. Unfortunately, at the moment, they're just drifting along like tumbleweeds.

> **PLAY TO YOUR STRENGTHS**
>
> When choosing a career, first pinpoint your skills and work preferences. That's the first step in choosing a job and building a career that makes you happy.

*You*, on the other hand, are about to become well informed so that you can make your own choice. Congratulations!

But before we can determine whether a career in business administration is right for you, we need to assess your own interests, skills, values, and personality.

## SELF-ASSESSMENT: PART 1

### Personality Trait Inventory

Five descriptive words appear in each of the following sets. In each set, circle the words that best describe you.

*Set One*

Calm, careful, cautious, methodical, organized

*Set Two*

Competitive, efficient, aggressive, adventurous, risk taker

*Set Three*

Friendly, outgoing, sincere, diplomatic, mature

*Set Four*

Trusting, stable, persevering, patient, loyal

*Set Five*

> Kind, modest, poised, reserved, reliable

## Self-Scoring Instructions

**Part One:** On a blank piece of paper, list all of the adjectives you circled. Next, try to come up with some more adjectives that describe you that weren't in any of the five sets above. Write down as many of these adjectives as you can think of. If your final list contains 20 or more adjectives, you know yourself well. If it contains 10 or fewer, you probably need to spend more time thinking about your attributes. The more you know about yourself, the better able you are to make career choices. If your list of adjectives is between 10 and 20, there's probably no need to spend more time evaluating yourself. Still, it's a good idea to be aware of your preferences and attitudes. Think about why you do what you do. It's a good way to learn more about YOU-know-who!

> **QUALITIES WORTH DEVELOPING**
>
> People who successfully pursue careers in business administration are easy to spot because they possess specific qualities, such as:
> - Makes decisions with confidence
> - Communicates well, both verbally and in writing
> - Adapts easily to change
> - Committed to lifelong learning
> - Willing to adopt a leadership role

**Part Two:** Think about how character traits impact career choices. Given the traits listed in each set above, do you agree they partner well with the positions offered below?

*Set One:* An accounting job

*Set Two:* A management position

*Set Three:* A job working with people, such as a financial planning or public relations job

*Set Four:* A job in public administration

*Set Five:* A job in banking

What other jobs can you think of that correspond with the traits in each set? (Note: There are no tricks here! *All* of the sets partner well with numerous positions in business administration.)

> **ENJOY WHAT YOU DO**
>
> While you may shine in a certain skill, you might not enjoy using it all the time. Avoid the trap of a job that requires heavy use of a skill or set of skills you don't like—even if people say you're a natural at it!

# SELF-ASSESSMENT: PART 2

## Work Environment Wish List

Rate each factor listed below on a scale of 1–3. (1 = A must-have! 2 = I can live with it, but it's not a preference. 3 = Forget about it; I'll keep searching.)

1. Clear-cut job description
2. Closely knit employee group
3. Desk job
4. Fast paced
5. Regular hours
6. Large company
7. Training programs
8. Periodic evaluations with chance for advancement
9. Job security
10. Given responsibility and empowered to act
11. Team player
12. Convenient work location
13. Flexible hours
14. Opportunity to travel
15. Lots of time on a computer
16. Work alone
17. Work with customers, clients, vendors
18. Creativity and initiative is rewarded
19. Train others
20. Predictable tasks each day/week/month
21. Always something new
22. Periodic job evaluations tied to merit increases in pay
23. Just here to pick up my paycheck
24. Fast lane open for advancement
25. Meaningful work
26. Excellent job benefits (i.e., medical insurance, vacations)

## Self-Scoring Instructions

Pay attention to the factors you rated number 1. Use these to start building a wish list describing your ideal work environment. If there are other factors that are important to you that weren't listed above, add those to your list, too.

Save your wish list. See if you rate factors the same way once you earn your degree. Be sure to think about this list when you hone in on a possible career. For example, you may not want to pursue work in public relations if the following factors don't make it onto your wish list: *team player; always something new; flexible hours.*

# WHERE CAN I LEARN MORE?

Use any search engine to find self-assessment exams developed by psychologists or other experts in this area.

- *www.discoveryourpersonality.com* contains information about Meyers-Briggs and other assessment devices.
- *www.careerexplorer.net* features skill and aptitude inventories. The site also posts articles written by experts on discovering your skills and work preferences.
- *www.UniversityOfLife.com* links you to personality profiles and skill inventories.

Does your high school guidance counselor or local community college have bona fide career or personality and attitude exams to administer? These may be available to you without cost. The best way to find out is to inquire.

Check library bookshelves, too. Two books that offer career planning and self-assessment data:

- *What Color Is Your Parachute? A Practical Manual for Job-Hunters & Career-Changers,* 2002, by Richard Nelson Bolles (Ten Speed Press, Berkeley, CA, 2001, $16.95). Updated annually, it's one of the best career-planning and self-assessment books. The job search and career-building techniques will serve you at any stage of your life.
- *Whistle While You Work: Heeding Your Life's Calling,* by Richard J. Leider and David A. Shapiro (Berrett-Koehler, San Francisco, CA, 2001, $15.95). The

book features case studies and worksheets and helps you identify work to match your gifts, aptitudes, passions, and values.

## GETTING STARTED

Let's assume you have the qualities to excel in one or more of the careers that are open to you in the field of business administration. You'll also want to know about:

- **Daily tasks.** What are they?
- **Salaries.** How much? How little?
- **Lifestyle.** Will you work in a city or a rural area? Must you be prepared to travel?
- **Personal satisfaction.** If you want more from your work than a paycheck, will these careers provide those opportunities?

**WORD TO THE WISE**

"We should all be concerned about the future because we will have to spend the rest of our lives there."

—C. F. Kettering, 1949

This little book takes you on a long journey in a short amount of time. It assists you to explore the many rewarding careers you can follow if you earn this degree. It alerts you to what you can expect from the career you target. It even tells you precisely how to obtain up-to-the-minute financial aid information for your education. Basically, this book paints the big picture and presents you with a magnifying glass!

The next move is yours. If you want a degree in business administration and all that goes with it, you've got the blueprint to use to make it happen. You're holding it in your hands.

The author, editors, and publisher take this opportunity to extend best wishes to you for your career success.

# Chapter One

# OPPORTUNITIES IN BUSINESS ADMINSTRATION: AN OVERVIEW

## FLEXIBLE CAREER OPTIONS

One of the biggest benefits of obtaining a degree in business administration: It's *a degree with maximum flexibility* that prepares you to excel in many different arenas. Make this degree yours and you'll have the ticket to a surprising number of rewarding careers in your hands.

Some possible occupations in business administration include:

- Accountant
- Advertising account executive
- Bank manager
- Business teacher
- Compensation/benefits administrator
- Consultant
- Entrepreneur
- Financial planner
- Financial aid director
- Hotel manager
- Human resources specialist
- Insurance broker

> **DIFFERENT CAREER PATHS, DIFFERENT BENEFITS**
>
> Not all business administration careers offer the same benefits. For example, entry-level earnings in accounting are typically thousands of dollars more than entry-level earnings in public relations. Look back at your Work Environment Wish List from the Introduction and decide which benefits are most important to you.

- Internal auditor
- Inventory control analyst
- IRS investigator
- Labor relations specialist
- Marketing/sales manager
- Marketing research analyst
- Nonprofit organization administrator
- Operations analyst/manager
- Property manager
- Public relations specialist
- Purchasing manager
- Restaurant manager
- Risk analyst
- Stockbroker
- Transportation director
- Urban/community planner
- Underwriter

. . . and many, many more!

Keep in mind that a newly earned degree in Business Administration enables you to get an *entry-level job*. You're not likely to become a tax advisor, for example, when you're just starting out in the business world. While you probably will not get everything you seek in an entry-level position, the job will allow you to gain experience, sending you in the right direction and helping you climb the ladder to future success. You should always focus on the idea that you are not just looking for a job; you are really building a *career*.


## FLEXIBLE EDUCATIONAL OPTIONS

You also have maximum flexibility in how you obtain your business degree. Do you want an associate's degree, a bachelor's degree, or even a graduate degree? Do you want to go to school full-time, part-time, or via the Internet? All of these options are available to you!

## Two, Four, Or More

- **Two years.** It's possible to earn an *associate's degree* in business administration by enrolling in a college that offers a two-year program of study.
- **Four years.** You can earn a *bachelor's degree* in business administration (sometimes referred to as a *baccalaureate degree*) by attending a college or university that offers a four-year program of study.
- **More.** After obtaining a bachelor's degree, another option opens up: an M.B.A., also known as a *master's degree in business administration*. This degree usually takes two years of full-time study (or four years of part-time study). Or, some schools offer a *combined degree*, so you can earn your bachelor's and master's degrees in a total of five years of full-time study.

The degree you earn (i.e., associate's, bachelor's, master's) will play a role in determining the entry-level job you can apply for within your chosen field and may also affect how high you can climb up the career ladder. A bank executive, for example, usually has at least a bachelor's degree in business administration. Admittedly, the degree alone won't earn him or her this executive position. It's also necessary to get on-the-job banking experience.

## Earn While You Learn

Many people hold a full-time job while going to school part-time—earning a good income while gaining valuable work experience. Or, if you can afford to, you can work part-time while going to school full-time. Another increasingly popular option is to work full-time while earning a business degree through distance education.

You'll have a better idea of which path meets your needs after you gather and evaluate information. The educational options available to you are discussed at length in chapter 4.

# THE FOUR MAIN FIELDS OF BUSINESS

Not all roads leading to a degree in business administration are the same. You may decide, for example, to concentrate on accounting because you enjoy working with numbers. The path you pursue will be different than that of someone who concentrates on marketing. Each of you will learn about the others' specialty, but each of you will concentrate on the kind of work you find most appealing.

---

> ### STOP AND THINK
>
> When researching career trends, stop and think about how the trends will affect you.
>
> - Is this information accurate today?
> - Does it apply in my region of the country?
> - Does bad news for management engaged in hiring staff represent good news for me (i.e., less job competition, more demand for my accounting skills)?
> - If improvements in the profession are underway now, will they be in place by the time I go job hunting?
>
> Don't be shy about asking questions. Follow up until you get the answers you need to make the best possible decisions.

> ### SOME POSSIBLE CAREERS IN ACCOUNTING
>
> Certified public accountant
>
> Internal auditor
>
> IRS agent
>
> Tax advisor
>
> Controller

You're about to examine four broad business fields: accounting, finance, marketing, and management. You'll be prepared to enter virtually any of them with a degree in business administration. By understanding a little about several careers, you're in a stronger position to narrow your choices and begin to focus on the studies and career that will suit you best. Be aware, however, that courses you take to earn this degree prepare you to excel in many different business arenas. So, if you know of a career in business administration that is not mentioned within these pages, use the resources listed (e.g., websites, professional associations) to obtain the information you seek.

# ACCOUNTING

What is **accounting**? The process of identifying, measuring, and communicating economic information to permit informed judgments and decisions by users of the information. (This definition comes from the American Accounting Association.)

## Employment Trends

Most accountant positions require at least a bachelor's degree in accounting or a related field. If you're considering a career in accounting, you should have an aptitude for mathematics and be able to analyze, compare, and interpret facts and figures quickly. You also need be able to clearly communicate the results of your work to clients and managers. You must be comfortable working with people, as well as with business systems and computers.

The field of accounting is experiencing sweeping changes as it transforms into a "knowledge services" profession. The next generation of accountants will have to know about bits, bytes, and e-commerce, along with knowing about debits and credits. They will have to be good planners (strategists) as well as good with numbers (statistics). Accountants who have earned professional recognition through certification or licensure will have the best job prospects.

According to Albert S. Williams, CPA, speaker and author of numerous articles, there has been a 20 percent decline in accounting majors in college, a decline in the number of CPA exam applicants, and a decline in interest among high school students in entering the profession. In his May 2001 article (the second in a series) entitled "The Accounting Profession's Labor Crisis: Damage Control," Williams spotlights four problem areas for accountants: salary and benefits, long hours, demanding work load, and a view of the work as a stepping stone to something else rather than a long-term career (e.g., employees leave to start their own practices). Mr. Williams believes this staff shortage is likely to get worse.

> **WHERE TO LOOK FOR MORE TRENDS**
>
> Use online search engines to find more info. Type in keywords such as these: *accounting profession trends*.

## Top Employers

There are so many small and middle-sized places of business that hire accountants it's virtually impossible to list them all. But mention "The Big 5" accounting firms and anyone "in the know" can name them: Ernst and Young (*www.eyi.com*), Arthur Andersen (*www.arthurandersen.com*), Deloitte and Touche (*www.deloitte.com*), KPMG (*www.kpmg.com*), and Price Waterhouse Coopers (*www.pwcglobal.com*). (But now, after the Enron debacle, there are really only "The Big 4" left, as Arthur Andersen, under federal indictment, struggles to survive.) Visit these firms' websites to learn more about each of these.

If you decide to pursue a career in accounting, you may want to work for a hospital, an insurance company, a large corporation, a government agency, or any one of a number of businesses. Large companies often have formal training programs and a blueprint that entry-level people can follow to advance. Small companies are usually less formal: After you're hired, a senior person will probably train you, and the path you follow to be successful is not as clearly defined. Obviously, there

> **MISSION STATEMENTS**
>
> - Why does a company do what it does?
> - How does a company do what it does?
> - What does a company stand for?
>
> Management addresses these questions in about 50 words or less in a document called a *mission statement*. Most companies post their mission statements on their websites. The sites also often feature an "About Our Company" webpage containing even more useful background information. Look up this information when you're researching a prospective employer: If you like what the company stands for, there's a better chance you'll like working for that company.

are pros and cons to seeking employment in either large or small places of business. Some possible pros and cons are listed below. Can you think of any others?

| **PRO: small accounting company** | **CON: small accounting company** |
| --- | --- |
| Advancement may be fast | Preparation for new assignments may be scanty |
| Mentor may help shape my future | I may have to navigate career on my own |
| Predictable client base | Limited exposure to new challenges |

### AN OPPORTUNITY FOR NETWORKING

Networking is the key to success in any career. Many professional organizations welcome students. You may be invited to attend workshops free of charge. If you attend general meetings, you can ask questions of working accountants who are able to give you real-life answers. Some professional organizations award scholarships. If you contact an organization's headquarters and don't find what you're looking for, ask for suggestions ("Can you direct me to an organization that might award scholarships?").

## Where Can I Learn More?

Professional organizations are a great source of information in any industry. Professional organizations serve members in various ways; for example, they may sponsor workshops and seminars, publish magazines that spotlight topics of interest to anyone in the industry, or conduct general meetings. Contacts made via a professional organization may lead to bringing in new business or finding skilled employees to hire.

There are hundreds of accounting organizations. Some are open to accountants doing business anywhere in the world, while others are open to accountants doing business within a particular state. Two accounting organizations are listed below:

- American Accounting Association (AAA), 5717 Bessie Drive, Sarasota, FL 34233-2399. Phone: (941) 921-7747. Website: *http://accounting.rutgers.edu/raw/aaa/*
- American Institute of Certified Public Accountants, 1211 Avenue of the Americas, New York, NY 10036. Website: *www.aicpa.org*

## FINANCE

What is **finance?** The science of the management of money and other assets. (The *American Heritage Dictionary* provides this definition at *www.dictionary.com.*) Finance is often broken down into three subindustries: banking, insurance, and securities and commodities. You can find information on any finance-related career that interests you by using your favorite search engine.

If you're thinking that finance isn't too different from accounting, you're correct. You'll need many of the same personality traits and work skills, such as having an aptitude for mathematics and good communication skills, and being detail-oriented and analytical. However, careers in finance take people in a different direction because the emphasis is on money management, investments, and credit, whereas accountants are more involved with the tracking and measurement of money.

Finance, insurance, and real estate employment increased by 13 percent from 1990 to 1999 in the United States, according to the U.S. Department of Labor. Most of this increase occurred in the late 1990s. Employment growth has been helped by the improved economic condition of financial institutions.

> **SOME POSSIBLE CAREER PATHS IN FINANCE**
>
> Financial planning
>
> Investment banking
>
> Corporate finance (e.g., establishing and monitoring employee retirement plans)
>
> Credit analysis
>
> Insurance underwriting
>
> Insurance sales
>
> Real estate

## Banking

### Employment Trends

Jobs available in banking include bill collectors, loan officers, trust officers, financial managers, branch managers, and securities, commodities, and financial services sales agents.

According to the Bureau of Labor Statistics, the banking industry employed over 2 million wage and salary workers in 1998, making it the largest industry in the finance, insurance, and real estate sector of the economy. More than 7 out of 10 jobs were in commercial banks; the remainder were concentrated in savings and loan associations and credit unions. The BLS predicts that employment in the banking industry is expected to increase 3 percent between 1998 and 2008. Much of the increase will occur in credit unions and small regional banks and savings institutions.

As banks diversify and begin offering new financial products, they will hire additional people with experience and skills to sell these new products. Banks will hire more trust officers to administer the estates of an aging population. Also, employment in human resources departments is expected to grow, as the need to train employees about new bank services and new regulations becomes more urgent.

### Top Employers

Most people know that banks safeguard money and valuables. They provide loans and administer payment services such as checking accounts, cashier's checks, and ATMs (automated teller machines). There are, however, different types of banks: *Commercial banks*, which offer a full range of services; *savings banks*, which cater mainly to savings and lending; *credit unions*, which conduct banking business for an exclusive group of people (e.g., teachers); and *Federal Reserve banks*, which primarily help regulate the banking industry. Federal Reserve banks, for example, make emergency loans to banks that are short of cash.

You'll probably recognize the names of these banking institutions: Bank of America (*www.bankofamerica.com*), Citibank (*www.citibank.com*), Chase Manhattan (*www.chase.com*), J.P. Morgan (*www.jpmorgan.com*), Mellon Bank (*www.mellon.com*), and Wells Fargo (*www.wellsfargo.com*). They are some of the large banking institutions doing business in the United States. Check out their websites for more information.

### Where Can I Learn More?

- Financial Executives International (FEI), 10 Madison Avenue, P.O. Box 1938, Morristown, NJ 07962-1938. Phone: (973) 898-4600. Website: *www.fei.org*
- American Bankers Association (ABA), 1120 Connecticut Avenue, NW, Washington, DC 20036. Phone: 1-800-BANKERS. Website: *www.aba.com*

## Insurance

### Employment Trends

Jobs available in insurance include claims adjusters, claims examiners, insurance investigators, underwriters, actuaries, and sales agents.

An article published in "Rough Notes" in 1999 discussed trends in the insurance industry and reported the industry was focusing on offering advice and as a result was entrenched in building "relationships." The writer observed that prior to this time, the insurance industry primarily offered products and services. (See: *http://library.northernlight.com*. Use keywords: *insurance industry trends.*)

The Bureau of Labor Statistics says that medical service and health insurance is the fastest growing sector of the insurance industry. However, while demand for insurance is expected to rise, job growth in some areas may be limited due to downsizing, productivity increases due to new technology, and a trend towards direct mail, telephone, and Internet sales.

## Top Employers

AFLAC (*www.aflac.com*), Aetna (*www.aetna.com*), Allstate (*www.allstate.com*), Blue Cross Blue Shield (*www.bluecares.com*), John Hancock (*www.jhancock.com*), Liberty Mutual (*www.libertymutual.com*), MetLife (*www.metlife.com*), and Northwestern Mutual (*www.northwesternmutual.com*) are just some of the many large insurance companies in the United States. Visit their websites to see the services they provide and the positions they're looking to fill.

Some major insurance companies are especially "student friendly" and offer intern positions to students and all kinds of assistance:

> **JOB HUNTING ONLINE**
>
> Want to see what kinds of jobs are available right now in finance? Check out these websites:
> - *www.jobsinthemoney.com*
> - *www.MyInsuranceCareer.com*
> - *www.ultimateinsurancejobs.com*

- Prudential Financial offers this advice online: "A career should be more than a progression to point B … It should be a journey where you chart destination … you initiate the movement … as you see fit. From internships and programs to extensive training, global opportunities and beyond, Prudential has the resources to take you anywhere. We invite you to explore our business and technology initiative and begin the journey." To learn more, check out *http://campus.prudential.com/campus*.

- Mutual of Omaha also has extensive information about "Planning For Your Career" online. See *www.mutualofomaha.com/careers*. You'll learn about actuarial internships, among other things. Questions regarding "Who's eligible?" are answered: "College students majoring in an actuarial-related field. Must have an aptitude for statistical interpretation and thorough background in Actuarial Science, Math, Statistics, Economics and/or Computer Science."

### Where Can I Learn More?

- American Insurance Association (AIA), 1130 Connecticut Avenue, NW, Suite 1000, Washington, DC 20036. Phone: (202) 828-7100. Website: *www.aiadc.org*

- *http://dmoz.org/Business/Insurance/Associations* has links to insurance associations from A–V.

## Securities and Commodities

### Employment Trends

The securities and commodities industry is made up of a variety of firms and organizations that bring together buyers and sellers of securities and commodities, manage investments, and offer financial advice. Jobs in this area include portfolio managers, retail brokers, floor brokers, brokerage clerks, financial planners, financial analysts, and financial managers.

The *Occupational Outlook Handbook* states that a number of professionals in this industry begin their careers as brokerage clerks. Depending on the actual job, brokerage clerks can be high school or college graduates. Clerks may be promoted to sales representative positions or other professional positions. A college education, although not essential, is increasingly important for securities, commodities, and financial services sales agents because it helps them to understand economic conditions and trends. Entry-level analyst and other managerial support positions usually are filled by college graduates who have majored in business administration, marketing, economics, accounting, industrial relations, or finance. Many of the large companies have management training programs for college graduates in which trainees work for brief periods in various departments to get a broad picture of the industry before they are assigned to a particular department.

> **CAREER ADVICE**
>
> At mutual funds, teamwork is a core value. If you're a loner and group activity is not what you do best, brokerage firms are where you should focus your job hunt.
>
> Source: *www.WetFeet.com*

Even though automated, online trading poses a long-term threat to brokerage employment levels, the securities and commodities industry will benefit as baby boomers save for retirement and a generally better educated and wealthier population requires investment advice. In addition, people are living longer and must plan to finance more years of retirement. According to *www.WetFeet.com*, this translates into a lot of jobs for brokers, and career growth and income can be excellent after your first three to five years. But those first few years of building a client base and learning the markets are difficult. There's little patience in this industry for either mediocre or incompetent performance resulting in slow or zero growth in client assets (and correspondingly in firm income from those assets).

## Top Employers

The securities and commodities industry employed 748,000 wage and salary workers in 2000, according to the BLS. An additional 125,000 workers were self-employed. The large, nationally known brokerage companies—many of which are headquartered in New York City—employ the majority of workers in this industry. Major players include Morgan Stanley Dean Witter (*www.msdw.com*), Merrill Lynch (*www.ml.com*), Goldman Sachs Group (*www.gs.com*), and Charles Schwab (*www.schwab.com*).

Many people also work for mutual fund management companies and smaller regional brokerage firms. Banks are becoming a factor in the industry: As a consequence of deregulation, many banks have been either acquiring securities firms or adding securities and commodities business to their list of services. A relatively small number of employees work at securities or commodities exchanges—primarily the New York Stock Exchange, the Chicago Board of Trade, the Chicago Mercantile Exchange, and a number of regional exchanges.

According to *www.WetFeet.com*, brokerage firms and mutual funds have invaded each other's turf in an ever-escalating financial-services war. In 1999, Congress repealed the 1933 Glass-Steagall Act, opening the door for banks, securities brokers, and insurance companies to engage in each other's formerly exclusive businesses, without restrictions. More consolidation of financial companies and of services within individual companies may follow.

## Where Can I Learn More?

- Securities Industry Association, 120 Broadway, 35th Floor, New York, NY 10271-0080. Phone: (212) 608-1500. Website: *www.sia.com*
- Association for Investment Management and Research (AIMR), P.O. Box 3668, 560 Ray C. Hunt Drive, Charlottesville, VA 22903-0668. Phone: 1-800-247-8132. Website: *www.aimr.org*
- Financial Planning Association, 3801 E. Florida Avenue, Suite 708, Denver, CO 80210. Phone: 1-800-322-4237. Website: *www.fpanet.org*

# MARKETING

What is **marketing**? The process of planning and executing the conception, pricing, promotion, and distribution of ideas, goods, and services to create exchanges that satisfy individual and organizational goals. (This definition comes from the American Marketing Association.)

---

**SOME POSSIBLE CAREERS IN MARKETING**

Public relations specialist

Advertising account manager

General sales

Media buyer

Market research

---

If you're considering a career in marketing, you need be able to communicate clearly and persuasively, both verbally and in writing. You should also have creativity, initiative, an outgoing personality, and an enthusiasm for motivating people.

Since there are so many possible careers that fall under this umbrella, it's not practical to list or discuss all of them here. Careers in public relations and advertising are discussed below. Use the resources mentioned below to obtain information about marketing-related careers or jobs that interest you.

## Public Relations

### *Employment Trends*

According to the Bureau of Labor Statistics, public relations specialists held about 137,000 jobs in 2000. About 60 percent of salaried public relations specialists worked in services industries—management and public relations firms, membership organizations, educational institutions, healthcare organizations, social service agencies, and advertising agencies. Others worked for communications firms, financial institutions, and government agencies. About 6 percent of public relations specialists were self-employed.

Most PR specialists have at least a bachelor's degree in marketing, business, communications, or a related field. Employment of public relations specialists is expected to increase rapidly, but keen competition is expected for entry-level jobs. Your best bet is to combine a bachelor's degree with a public relations internship or other related work experience.

In public relations firms, you might be hired as a research assistant or account assistant and then be promoted to account executive, account supervisor, vice president, and eventually, senior vice president. A similar career path is followed in corporate public relations, although the titles may be different.

### Top Employers

Check out the websites of some of the big PR firms, such as Weber Shandwick (*www.webershandwick.com*), Edelman PR Worldwide (*www.edelman.com*), Fleishman-Hillard (*www.fleishman-hillard.com*), and Ruder Finn (*www.ruderfinn.com*).

It would be a mistake to stop there, because public relations jobs are found in virtually every industry. Motor vehicle dealers, printers and publishers, retail chains, and the entertainment industry usually have major public relations departments. If you enjoy fashion, you can move your public relations career in that direction. If you have a passion for racing cars, you can move your public relations career in that direction. Sports? There's practically no end to the choices you can make.

> **DID YOU KNOW?**
>
> Public relations specialists employed by the government may be called *press secretaries, information officers, public affairs specialists,* or *communications specialists.* Unofficially, they're often known as *spin doctors.*

Large companies may put newly hired business administration degree holders on the fast track for advancement by placing them in management training programs. These pro-grams may be designed and operated in collaboration with marketing and advertising associations, which focus on professional development for their own members. A large company may also permit you to attend courses during paid work hours and may even pay for your courses when you complete them successfully. At the same time, if you accept a position within a smaller company and work with the owner or another talented person who makes the company a success, you'll have an excellent role model mentoring you and helping to train you one-on-one.

> **READ WHAT THE EXPERTS READ**
>
> It's not surprising that people working in a public relations career communicate widely with one another through websites and publications. Communication is their business! If you have a company in mind that you'd like to work for, you can probably learn which publications the public relations staff favors. If the company subscribes to *PR & Marketing Network,* for example, that's the publication you should review.

### Where Can I Learn More?

- Public Relations Society of America (PRSA),
  33 Irving Place, New York, NY 10003-2376.
  Website: *www.prsa.org*. PRSA Chapters are scattered around the country.
  Look for similar associations based in your home state or the state where you

hope to work. The industry in which you work as a public relations specialist will probably dictate the professional association that will best serve you.

- *www.odwyerpr.com*. O'Dwyer's PR Daily is a comprehensive website that offers "online access to the inside news of public relations." A must-see for anyone who is considering a PR career.
- *www.public-relations-online.net/publications*. Public Relations Online is another excellent reference source for the PR industry.

## Advertising

### Employment Trends

Advertising agencies write copy and prepare artwork, graphics, and other creative work, and then place the resulting ads on television or radio or in newspapers, magazines, or other advertising media. Traditionally, advertising agencies break activities into four categories: account management, media, research, and creative. (These days there's also Internet advertising, which created the need for still another department.)

Beginners usually enter the industry in the account management or media department. But if you think you might enjoy working in an advertising agency, by all means examine all possible job descriptions. (Remember, your degree in business administration prepares you to walk through both traditional and newly designed doors!) Typical entry-level positions include: assistant account executive, assistant art director, assistant copywriter, assistant media planner, and assistant media buyer.

According to the Bureau of Labor Statistics, employment in advertising is expected to grow 32 percent over the next ten years, compared with 15 percent for all industries combined. However, the competition for entry-level jobs is unusually fierce in this "glamour" industry. Your best bet is to combine a bachelor's degree with an internship in an ad agency or other work-related experience.

### Top Employers

Advertising is less flexible than many other industries in terms of location: Employment is concentrated in a few large cities. New York City is the undisputed adver-

---

**DID YOU KNOW?**

According to the Bureau of Labor Statistics:

- Approximately 4 out of 5 advertising firms employ fewer than 10 employees.
- Opening your own firm is considered a good way to advance your career in the advertising industry.

tising capital; other top locations include Chicago, Detroit, Los Angeles, San Francisco, Boston, Minneapolis, and Dallas.

Some large, full-service advertising agencies include: Ogilvy & Mather (*www.ogilvy.com*), J. Walter Thompson (*www.jwtworld.com*), D'Arcy Masius Benton & Bowles (*www.dmbb.com*), DDB Needham (*www.ddbn.com*), and Grey Advertising (*www.grey.com*). Visit their websites to learn more about these agencies.

You may think that an advertising executive works exclusively in an advertising agency. Omit the word *exclusively* and you are correct. Many companies have divisions that produce and place their own advertising. The advertising industry also includes firms that sell advertising space for publications, radio, television, and the Internet.

### Where Can I Learn More?

- American Association of Advertising Agencies, 405 Lexington Avenue, New York, NY 10174. Website: *www.aaaa.org*
- American Advertising Federation, 1101 Vermont Avenue, NW, Suite 500, Washington, DC 20005-6306. Website: *www.aaf.org*

## MANAGEMENT

What is **management**? The manner of treating, directing, carrying on, or using for a purpose; administration; guidance; control; judicious use of means to accomplish an end. (This is part of the definition provided by *Webster's Revised Unabridged Dictionary* at *www.dictionary.com*.) As you know, managers are needed in all areas of business. Managers also work in nonprofit organizations and in the government.

If you're considering a career in management, you should have good communication skills and be able to establish effective working relationships with many different people. You must be adept at multitasking, problem solving, and coping with deadlines. You should also be analytical, detail oriented, flexible, and decisive.

**SOME POSSIBLE CAREER PATHS IN MANAGEMENT**

Public administration
Office management
Retail management
Human resources
Facility management
Sports management
Arts management
Consulting

---

**HAVING THE RIGHT BACKGROUND**

While some managers in the public sector have a background in business administration, many have a background related to their jobs. For example, school superintendents and principals usually start out as teachers and often get a master's degree in education administration rather than a degree in business administration.

---

Since there are so many different careers that fall under the management umbrella, it's not practical to list or discuss all of them here. Management careers in government and administrative services are discussed below.

## Public Administration

### Employment Trends

Having a degree in business or public administration is helpful if you want a career that involves establishing government policy and developing laws, rules, and regulations. Public administration covers the gamut of government positions, including governors, lieutenant governors, city managers, district managers, revenue directors, and legislators. Competition for jobs can be keen because the number of these positions generally remains fairly stable. Many graduates with public administration degrees decide to pursue careers in the nonprofit and private sectors.

The Bureau of Labor Statistics points out that working in management support positions in government is a great way to get the experience and personal contacts required to eventually secure a position as a manager. For example, you can gain experience as a management analyst or an assistant in government departments working for committees, councils, or chief executives. In this capacity, you will learn about planning, budgeting, and other aspects of running a government. With sufficient experience, a smaller community may hire you as a town, city, or county manager. Advancement often takes the form of securing positions in progressively larger towns, cities, or counties. A broad knowledge of current events, combined with communication skills and the ability to compromise, are essential for advancement in this field.

---

**DID YOU KNOW?**

According to the BLS:

- More than half of all federal workers hold managerial or professional jobs—double the rate for the workforce as a whole.
- About 4 out of 5 federal employees work outside the Washington, DC metropolitan area.
- About 5 percent of federal employees are assigned overseas, mostly in embassies or defense installations.

---

In the federal government, managerial workers include a broad range of officials who, at the highest levels, may head federal agencies or programs. Middle managers, on the other hand, usually oversee one activity or aspect of a program. Advancement in the federal government is commonly based on a system of occupational pay levels, or "grades." Workers enter the federal civil service at the starting grade for an occupation and begin a career ladder of promotions.

### Top Employers

In addition to the federal government and the 50 state governments, there are about 87,000 local governments, according to the Bureau of the Census. Employment can also be found in independent agencies such as the Social Security Administration (SSA), the Securities and Exchange Commission (SEC), the Federal Communications Commission (FCC), and the Environmental Protection Agency (EPA).

> **JOB OPENINGS**
>
> - Curious about what types of jobs are available in your state government? Check out *www.csg.org/ other_resources/classifieds.html* to see current job openings.
> - Information on obtaining a position with the Federal government is available from the Office of Personnel Management (OPM). Visit *www.usajobs.opm.gov* or call (478) 757-3000.

### Where Can I Learn More?

- American Society for Public Administration, 1120 G Street, NW, Suite 700, Washington, DC 20005. Website: *www.aspa.org*
- Council of State Governments, P.O. Box 11910, Lexington, KY 40578-1910. Website: *www.csg.org*
- National League of Cities, 1301 Pennsylvania Avenue, NW, Washington, DC 20004-1763. Website: *www.nlc.org*

## Administrative Services Management

### Employment Trends

Workers in this field plan, direct, or coordinate the many services that allow organizations to operate efficiently, such as secretarial and reception, administration, payroll, conference planning and travel, information and data processing, mail, materials scheduling and distribution, printing and reproduction, records, and telecommunications.

According to the BLS, entry-level requirements in this field vary by job responsibility. For first-line administrative services managers of secretarial, mailroom, and related support activities, many employers prefer an associate degree in business or management, although a high school diploma may suffice when combined with appropriate experience. Managers of more complex services, such as contract administration, generally need at least a bachelor's degree in business, human resources, or finance.

Most administrative services managers in small organizations advance by moving to other management positions or to a larger organization. Getting a master's degree in business administration or a related field enhances a first-level manager's opportunities to advance to a mid-level management position, such as director of administrative services, and eventually to a top-level management position, such as executive vice president for administrative services.

The BLS predicts that corporate restructuring and increasing utilization of office technology may result in a flatter organizational structure with fewer levels of management, reducing the need for some middle management positions over the next 10 years. However, administrative services managers employed in management services and management consulting will be in demand, as public and private organizations continue to contract out and streamline their administrative services functions in an effort to cut costs.

> **OPERATION ENTERPRISE**
>
> Operation Enterprise is a program created by the American Management Association for high school and college students interested in careers in management. Taught by AMA faculty and senior executives, OE provides valuable leadership and communication skills that are essential for success. Students are eligible for 3 semester hours of undergraduate credit after completing the program, which includes roundtable discussions, team exercises, and business simulations. For more info, call 1-800-634-4262 or visit *www.amanet.org/oe/index.htm*.

### *Top Employers*

Administrative services managers are found in virtually every industry. According to the BLS, administrative services managers held about 362,000 jobs in 2000. About half worked in service industries, including engineering and management, business, education, social, and health services.

### *Where Can I Learn More?*

- American Management Association, 1601 Broadway, New York, NY 10019-7420. Website: *www.amanet.org*
- National Management Association, 2210 Arbor Blvd., Dayton, OH 45439. Website: *www.nma1.org*

# Chapter Two

# ENTRY-LEVEL OPPORTUNITIES

Now that you know about the unlimited career opportunities in business administration, you're probably thinking, "OK, where do I start?"

## THE INSIDE STORY FROM CAREER COUNSELORS

Because there are so many exciting careers available in the various areas of business administration, you might need some one-on-one help to decide which career is right for you. Or, on the other end of the spectrum, once you've chosen a career and received your training, you might want some expert advice on how to land your first job. Enter the career counselor! Career counselors spend their working hours assisting people to make decisions and carry out plans related to career directions. In a moment, we'll examine some of the collective wisdom that career counselors have offered about getting a job and what you can expect from an entry-level position.

But first, it's important to realize that not all career counselors have the same training or background. If you seek assistance from a counselor, you'll want to know something about that person.

### Finding a Good Career Counselor

Like many professionals, career counselors can obtain professional certification as proof of their professionalism and reliability. A *National Certified Career Counselor* designation indicates that the person who assists you has:

1. A graduate degree in counseling or a related field from an accredited learning institution.

2. Completed supervised counseling experience

3. Worked at full-time career development work for a minimum of three years

4. Successfully completed a knowledge-based certification examination.

For a list of National Certified Career Counselors in your state, contact:

- National Career Development Association, 10820 E. 45th Street, Suite 210, Tulsa, Oklahoma 74146. Phone: (866) 367-6232. Website: *http://ncda.org*
- National Board for Certified Counselors (NBCC), 3 Terrace Way, Suite D, Greensboro, NC 27403-3660. Phone: (336) 547-0607. Website: *www.nbcc.org*

Some State Licensure Boards license career counselors to practice. You should be able to obtain names of practitioners from a State Licensure Board if you're searching for a counselor. If you scan the telephone book Yellow Pages under Career Counseling, look for certification or license information in a counselor's listing.

> **VIRTUAL COUNSELING**
>
> At San Diego State University in California, career counselors are introduced online (*http://career.sdsu.edu*). If this is of interest to you, see whether the college you're planning to attend does the same.

It's also good to know that career counseling services may be available to you via the college you're planning to attend. It's unlikely you'll be asked to pay fees for these services beyond your tuition fee. At the same time, services may differ from those you obtain via a private practitioner.

It's wise to ask any potential counselor for details about costs and how you will benefit from their services before you get started.

## GETTING YOUR FOOT IN THE DOOR

### Never Underestimate a Good Résumé

Your application for any position—whether it's an entry-level job or an internship or co-op position—starts with a good résumé that presents you in a manner that maximizes all of your skills and ability, experience, and achievements. A good résumé is a good sales presentation—much like a newspaper ad for any product, such as a car or a refrigerator. It attracts attention and creates interest in wanting to see you for an interview. So pay attention to the text and appearance of your résumé: It represents you and is the first contact with a prospective employer. Remember: You don't get a second chance to make a good first impression!

Writing a good résumé is a subject in itself. You will find many books in libraries and bookstores that give helpful suggestions for writing résumés. These books can tell you what to put into them and what not to put into them, but, in the end, the task of putting it into words is all yours. There are professional services that will compose a résumé for you, with varying degrees of competency, charging anywhere from $50 to $200 or more for a compete package, including a cover letter.

You can submit your résumé in several ways:

1. Copy and paste your résumé and cover letter into the body of an email message. If you do this, changes in formatting may occur: Line breaks and tabs may change, and certain characters such as bullets may not translate, resulting in a document that's difficult to read.

2. Send your résumé as an email attachment. However, there are problems with this method because some companies will not accept attachments for fear of viruses. But if an employer specifies that you can send a word-processed résumé, go ahead and attach it to your email message.

3. Submit an ASCII Text résumé. This is simply a text résumé without fancy formatting, such as bold face, italics, certain fonts, and sizes over 12 point. It is advantageous because it is recognizable by nearly every application and every computer, even if it is not the prettiest format.

4. Go the old-fashioned route and mail or fax your résumé.

With a good résumé, you ought to be receiving some responses to your applications, if you are realistic about the type and level of jobs for which you are applying. But a résumé doesn't usually get you the job. Generally, nobody hires you from a piece of paper. They'll want to meet with you in person to determine what kind of person you are and whether they like you and want to work with you. Your next step: the interview.

## Appearance Counts

Your choice of clothing tells the interviewer something about your judgment and suggests how you view the company and the opportunity. If you're well groomed and dressed in a manner that suggests business as opposed to leisure/play, it's taken as a sign of respect for yourself and the people with whom you are interviewing. Your grooming and choice of clothing suggest to the interviewer whether or not you'll "fit" into the company. Even if casual dress is acceptable for employees, remember that you're not an employee (yet!).

*Illustration:* Two high school seniors are interviewed for a summer job position at a local public relations firm. Charlie arrives dressed in well-pressed slacks and a dress shirt and has obviously spent time polishing his shoes. Tom arrives in jeans and a T-shirt and is wearing athletic shoes. Each student is clean, well groomed, well spoken, and eager to get the position. The department manager doesn't need more than one minute to make a decision once the interviews end: Charlie is hired.

> **LASTING IMPRESSIONS**
>
> Like it or not, people tend to judge a book by its cover. If you want to make a good impression, pay careful attention to your personal appearance.

## Do Your Homework

What do you know about the company or organization? If you don't know something about the company's history, track record, or mission, you aren't likely to make an interviewer believe that you want the job.

*Illustration:* Brittany, a high school senior, arrives to discuss an internship with a manager of an accounting firm but quickly demonstrates she doesn't realize that it's an international firm and most of the company's clients are in the entertainment industry. When she's asked, "Why do you want to work here?" Brittany replies, "I want accounting experience serving small businesses so that I'm better prepared to do that when I get my degree." It is a good answer, but not at this company! The manager thanks her for coming and keeps searching for an intern.

## Represent Yourself Accurately

It may be tempting to make an interviewer believe that you've had more experience or more training than you've actually had. Don't do it!

*Illustration*: Drake has worked in his father's wholesale produce business since he was twelve years old. While interviewing for a customer service job in a department store, he tells the interviewer that he is good with people and brags that he has extensive sales experience. "I usually get customers to buy more items than they planned to buy. It's called suggestive selling." Instead of hiring Drake for a job in customer service, the interviewer offers him a job in sales, explaining, "Our sales team earns minimum wage and gets sales commissions." Drake accepts the interviewer's offer. Everyone he works with likes him, but he doesn't have much sales success. His supervisor encourages him to keep trying, but Drake is disappointed with his earnings and soon leaves to look for another job.

## Be Careful What You Say

Some people get especially chatty when they feel anxious, and some folks do just the opposite. Concentrate on answering questions you're asked. Don't deliver one-word answers, but don't volunteer information unless you believe it will help you get what you want.

> **WHO ARE YOU?**
>
> Try this exercise before you start going out on job interviews: Put down on paper the reasons someone should hire you and where you want to progress in the next few years and after five or ten years. Start with an outline format, and then use your outline to write a two-page personal statement. Besides being a great writing exercise, this will help prepare you for some of the questions the interviewer may ask.

*Illustration*: Ms. Gould is seated at the receptionist's desk when Barry arrives early to talk with Mr. Sikes about a summer job. She invites Barry to take a chair, and when she isn't answering the telephone, she asks Barry questions about his future. "I really like cars," he says. "I hope I can get into a career where I can use what I know about cars." Ms. Gould laughs, "That's helpful here since our company owns and operates carwashes." Barry chats with her about the latest car models. He talks about making money by polishing cars for friends and neighbors since he was ten years old. He goes on to say how he likes being active and hates being chained to a desk. Finally, Mr. Sikes invites Barry into his office for the interview. Mr. Sikes explains that the position is in the accounting department and Barry would be seated at a computer most of the day, setting up spreadsheets and entering data. It is a position that could lead to an internship with the company, and Barry hopes to parlay this "foot in the door" into a long-term relationship with the company. His enthusiasm and command of general knowledge impress Mr. Sikes greatly. When Barry leaves the office, he says good-bye to his new friend, Ms. Gould. In the end, Barry isn't offered the job. Was another job candidate better qualified? Or did Ms. Gould tell Mr. Sikes that Barry didn't like sitting at a desk? Barry will never know. He does know that he probably said too much.

*Alert!* On the other hand … don't be short-sighted. When you apply for a job or a student loan or a school, if you're pretty sure that something about it is "awful," you probably shouldn't go further. Maybe Barry was better off not getting a job offer from Mr. Sikes. He may have hated the job! Even though he wanted to use it as a stepping-stone to an internship with the company, he might have been miserable seated at a desk working on spreadsheets and entering data each and every day. When that happens, it's generally not possible to do your best.

## CRITERIA TO CONSIDER WHEN CHOOSING AN EMPLOYER

What matters most to students preparing to enter the workforce? A survey of nearly 1,000 prospective and recent college graduates revealed the following criteria:

| Criterion | Percent of Respondents |
|---|---|
| Opportunity for advancement | 45 percent |
| Good benefits package | 34 percent |
| Continuing ed/training opportunities | 33 percent |
| Starting salary offers | 31 percent |
| Job duties | 29 percent |
| Geographic location | 25 percent |
| Employees being treated with honesty and fairness | 24 percent |
| Stability | 22 percent |
| Ethical business practices | 13 percent |
| Personnel you will work with | 13 percent |
| Embraces diversity | 11 percent |
| Casual atmosphere | 7 percent |
| Social conscience | 5 percent |
| Recognized name | 4 percent |
| Size of company | 2 percent |
| Signing bonus | 1 percent |

*Source: National Association of Colleges and Employers 2001 Graduating Student and Alumni Survey*

## Remember What "Entry-Level" Means

While the duties involved in entry-level positions vary depending upon the career or field you're in, entry-level jobs in general tend to be predictable. Tune in to these realities and you'll shed false expectations and avoid disappointments.

1. You'll need to learn about the company and how to perform your job. This takes time. A long-time employee may train you or you may be expected to participate in a training program.

2. You'll have limited authority to act.

3. Starting salaries are likely to be the lowest salaries in this career or field. If you've been looking at industry averages, you'll want to remember entry-level wages aren't "average" wages. There's one exception to consider. If you have internship or co-op work experience on your résumé, according to data on *www.jobweb.com*, you will earn an 8.9 percent larger starting salary over a new hire with no experience.

> **REALISTIC EXPECTATIONS**
>
> By the time you leave college with your degree and become an employee in your field of endeavor, you're probably ready to take on the world. Relax! It's not often that someone fresh out of college is given major responsibilities in a company.

4. You probably will be considered a trial employee for the first 30, 60, or 90 days. Trial employees may not be entitled to medical coverage or other benefits.

5. Prior to becoming a permanent employee, you may be dismissed without notice. If you've moved to a new home in order to accept this job, you'll want to be cautious about signing a long-term lease or making other long-term commitments.

6. Co-workers may not welcome your arrival. It's possible that you're filling a position that someone in-house wanted. It's possible that co-workers don't like change. Some may resent having to train you or resent the fact that you're likely to slow things down. It's possible that people have formed cozy circles that keep newcomers outside. While you're adjusting to the new job and want to put your best foot forward, this challenge is not one you need! Relax. It may be simply a matter of more time needed for co-workers to get to know you and accept you. That works both ways: You may need time to get to know co-workers better before you feel comfortable.

7. You'll ask questions. Different people may give you different answers. When that happens, be alert to actions rather than words. Observe how thing are accomplished. There may be more than one way to accomplish the same goal. If in doubt, check with your boss.

8. Managing your time away from work can be a challenge. When you're in an entry-level position, you may be more exhausted because you expend so much energy

getting adjusted. (The same thing can happen when you first leave home and live in a dormitory or get your own apartment.) You may have to travel a new route to get to and from the workplace. Does the dry cleaner close too early? Does that prevent you from having a suit or skirt ready for a special meeting? You may need to use a new dry cleaner. All of the little things that support everyday activities may need to be fine-tuned.

## Keep Your Eye on the Prize

If you get discouraged, remember that you won't be stuck in an entry-level position forever. Once your boss has confidence in your work, he or she will start giving you more challenging assignments.

*Illustration*: Sara, a recent college graduate with a bachelor's degree in Business Administration, gets a job with a large public relations firm. The firm is based in Boston and her starting salary is $23,000 a year. (Sara's manager earns $46,000 a year.) As a beginner, she scans newspapers and magazines for articles having anything to do with the company's clients. She maintains information files. She helps with new business efforts by conducting research (e.g., obtaining demographic data). Sara helps to maintain media lists. She monitors the firm's website daily. She has the authority to notify the webmaster to make changes if she sees dated material online. She attends staff meetings. She participates in a 14-day training program and afterward is assigned to write press releases. Since her firm writes speeches for clients, Sara is assigned to work with a senior speechwriter. Sara is a self confident, outgoing person. She enjoys public speaking, solving problems, and writing.

After nine months, she's no longer considered an entry-level employee. Instead of a 35-hour workweek, she generally works at least 40 hours a week. Sara works some weekends, especially when clients open new stores, make television appearances, launch new products at shopping malls, or sponsor sporting events. Her salary remains the same, but Sara now has entitlements such as sick leave with pay. She's eligible to participate in the company's medical and dental plans.

Eventually, Sara will travel to meet with clients and government officials. She will coach clients before they make public appearances and will help hire and train entry-level employees. Few of her entry-level tasks will be part of her day-to-day routine.

# QUIZ: DO YOU KNOW HOW TO GET AHEAD?

This quiz is designed to make you think about positioning yourself for success. You might think it is premature because you haven't earned your degree. Still, by participating in this quiz, you're learning more about yourself and about the realities of life as an entry-level worker.

Read the following questions and assume you have an entry-level job. Read each of the answers and select the best one. See how well you score.

1. I've been working for the company for six weeks and I'm treated like I don't know anything. I'm going to:
   a) Ask for more responsibility.
   b) Wait and see what happens.
   c) Quit.

2. I feel foolish asking so many questions. I'm going to:
   a) Ask anyway. (Eventually, I'll know more.)
   b) Make my own decisions and act.
   c) Wait for someone else to ask.

3. I accepted this job for a low salary and now I'm sorry. It's time to:
   a) Demonstrate my value to the company so I can ask for a raise.
   b) Ask for a raise.
   c) Quit and find a better paying entry-level job.

4. I don't think I can do this job. Why did they hire me?
   a) The "boss" thinks I can do the job.
   b) I fooled everyone.

5. I don't like the long commute to work. I'd better:
   a) Keep this job for a minimum of one year.
   b) Let the boss know I'm leaving because of the long commute.
   c) Find an apartment closer to work.

6. I know more than my boss knows about computers. It might be a good idea to:

   a) Tell my boss about my computer experience.

   b) Just play dumb.

## Scoring Your Responses

If you picked all *a* answers, you score 6 out of 6. Congratulations for knowing how to position yourself for success! If you selected *b* or *c* answers, look at the question(s) again and ask yourself why *a* is the better answer. Consider the following:

- Asking for responsibility announces that you want to be productive.

- Asking questions is part of the learning process. (But be a good listener, too.)

- Don't accept a job if the wages are inadequate. If you do, however, try to stay with the company for at least one year. Otherwise, the next employer may wonder why you left so soon.

- Don't waste time talking to yourself unless you're sending positive messages. If you have a positive attitude, most things are possible!

- When you accepted the job, you accepted responsibility for working at that location. Resign yourself to a long commute or move closer to the office, but stay with it. It demonstrates commitment and strength of character. These qualities help position you for success.

- Why waste everyone's time being trained for something you already know? At the same time, you'll want to be tactful when you mention your skill.

Notice how some of the comments you've just read can also be applied to earning a degree in business administration? Adapt these strategies now and position yourself for success in school, too!

# Chapter Three

# CAREER CLOSE-UPS

In chapter 1, we discussed various broad fields in business administration. In this chapter, we're going to take a closer look at some of the careers that you can enter with a degree in business administration. But first, we need to discuss two important concepts that play a central role in any job search: job descriptions and salary requirements.

## JOB DESCRIPTIONS

Job descriptions define the responsibilities of a specific job. Human resources employees generally write and maintain them. Job descriptions are important to management because they serve as a guide when hiring employees and later when it's time to evaluate performance. For example, if a job description calls for a command of specific computer software programs and the job candidate doesn't have this know-how, he or she shouldn't be hired for that job.

You may not see an official job description until you're hired, but well-written "help wanted" job listings will describe the job.

*Illustration:* **Assistant to the City Manager** is the heading on an advertisement appearing on the Internet at *www.craigslist.org*. In addition to mentioning the city name, annual salary, and educational requirements, it states: "This position will play a key role in planning and coordinating city public information and community relations programs, providing staff support to city council committees, citizen advisory groups and committees and commissions, and analyzing a wide variety of technical and complex public policy issues."

At another website (*www.job-interview.net/sample/Mgmtsamp.htm*), a simulated job interview for an **Assistant City Manager** is presented. In the process, a partial job description is included: "The responsibilities of the city manager's office staff; direction of administrative and internal operational services of the city; budget development; city council staff support; agenda development … The Assistant also serves as the city manager in the city manager's absence."

If you didn't know what a city manager's assistant did … you do now! You may decide this isn't the kind of work you want to do. Or, you may be thrilled to discover such a job exists. Bring on that degree in business administration!

## SALARY EXPECTATIONS

What kind of earnings can you expect? The answer to this question may cause you to select or reject a particular career. Find out now and you won't be in for a rude awakening.

Salaries are influenced by factors such as geographic location and cost of living (i.e., rent, food, transportation). Cost of living in a big city is usually more expensive than in smaller towns. Employers take that into consideration when hiring. General economic conditions (i.e., recession, inflation) and your education, skills, and experience are factors, too. Then there's supply and demand. Are there lots of people looking for work who can do the job? If so, employers offer less money when hiring. When few skilled people are available, employers are willing to pay big bucks to fill that position.

> **KEY TERM**
>
> **Median annual earnings** refers to the boundary between the highest paid 50 percent and lowest paid 50 percent of workers in an occupation (i.e., half the workers earn more than the median and half earn less).

Many people ignore the fact that the benefits a company provides are part of their earnings, too. Health insurance and dental insurance are expensive if you have to purchase them yourself. And if you didn't have a job, you wouldn't be entitled to two weeks of paid vacation, would you?

*Illustration:* Howard worked as a summer-hire for an osteopathic foundation directly after high school and during the summers before his sophomore and junior years at college. He was planning to earn a degree in business administration and was interested in a career in marketing. During the summers, he was provided with housing and living assistance in addition to his salary.

When key staff members went on vacations, Howard stepped into their jobs. Of course, he did this under the direction of the foundation's operations manager. She knew he was interested in marketing, and when the marketing director left for a four-week vacation, she permitted Howard to perform about 80 percent of the marketing director's tasks. During that time, Howard attended meetings with vendors, approved magazine copy for the printer, hired a writer to write an article, and went on location with an independent contractor to set up photography shoots.

The operations manager told Howard that his chances of getting a full-time job offer anywhere would increase by more than 50 percent because of his summer work experience. Howard calculated that had a dollar value, too: If he got a job offer in May instead of June, that would result in four or five weeks more of income instead of outgo as he pounded the pavement interviewing and looking for a job.

It was agreed that if Howard took a job with the foundation after graduation, the time he worked during the summers would be counted toward full-time job service. This meant he would be eligible for healthcare, holiday pay, and other benefits much earlier than usual.

## AN INSIDE LOOK AT CAREERS IN BUSINESS ADMINISTRATION

The career close-ups that follow will give you a better understanding of jobs in business administration and a fuller idea of what they require. You'll also see what we mean when we say that a degree in business administration will open doors to jobs that will satisfy *any* interest. We will examine just a handful of the many careers available in the four main business fields we discussed in chapter 1: accounting, finance, marketing, and management.

Note that each close-up includes a "career ladder" listing—an example of where you can go after getting enough experience to broaden your job responsibilities and increase your income. After all, you're not just trying to find a job that interests you—you want to build a solid, rewarding career!

# ACCOUNTING CAREERS

## Public Accountant

### Work Environment Wish List

Go back and check your Work Environment Wish List from the Introduction to this book. Did you rate any of the following characteristics as a "must-have"? If so, you might be a good candidate for a job as a public accountant.

- Desk job
- Regular hours
- Periodic evaluations with chance for advancement
- Given responsibility and empowered to act
- Team player
- Lots of time on a computer
- Work with customers, clients, vendors
- Fast lane open for advancement
- Excellent job benefits

### Salary Range

Associate accountant: $25,000–$38,000

Senior accountant: $33,000–$52,000

Manager: $45,000–$74,000

(Source: *www.WetFeet.com*)

### Duties and Responsibilities

Public accountants, many of whom are Certified Public Accountants (CPAs), generally have their own businesses or work for public accounting firms. Public accountants perform a broad range of activities for their clients, who may be corporations, governments, nonprofit organizations, or individuals. For example, some public accountants concentrate on tax matters, such as advising companies of the tax advantages and disadvantages of certain business decisions and preparing individual income tax returns. Others may audit clients' financial statements and report to investors and authorities that the statements have been correctly prepared and reported.

Accountants also are increasingly assuming the role of a personal financial advisor. They not only provide clients with accounting and tax help, but also help them develop a personal budget, manage assets and investments, plan for retirement, and recognize and reduce exposure to risks.

Computers are rapidly changing the nature of the work for most accountants and auditors. With the aid of special software packages, accountants summarize transactions in standard formats for financial records and organize data in special formats for financial analysis.

### What You Need to Succeed

You need to be good at math and able to analyze, compare, and interpret facts and figures quickly. You must be good at working with people and with computers. And because millions of financial statement users rely on their services, accountants should have high standards of integrity.

Most public accountant positions require at least a bachelor's degree in accounting or a related field. CPAs will have the best job prospects. All States use the four-part Uniform CPA Examination prepared by the American Institute of Certified Public Accountants (AICPA). The 2-day CPA examination is rigorous, and only about one-quarter of those who take it each year pass every part they attempt. The vast majority of states require CPA candidates to be college graduates, but a few states substitute work experience for a college degree.

### The Inside Scoop

Graduates of junior colleges and correspondence schools, as well as bookkeepers and accounting clerks who meet the education and experience requirements set by their employers, can obtain junior accounting positions and advance to positions with more responsibilities by demonstrating their accounting skills on the job.

### Career Ladder

Entry-level public accountants (often called associate or staff accountants) usually start by assisting with work for several clients. You may advance to a position with more responsibility in one or two years, and to a senior accountant position within another few years. If you excel, you could become a supervisor, manager, or partner; open your own public accounting firm; or transfer to an executive position in management accounting or internal auditing in a private firm.

# FINANCE CAREERS

## Financial Planner

### Work Environment Wish List

Go back and check your Work Environment Wish List from the Introduction to this book. Did you rate any of the following characteristics as a "must have"? If so, you might be a good candidate for a job as a financial planner.

- Closely knit employee group
- Given responsibility and empowered to act
- Flexible hours
- Opportunity to travel
- Lots of time on a computer
- Work with customers, clients, vendors
- Creativity and initiative is rewarded

### Salary Range

Median annual earnings in the industries employing the largest number of financial planners in 2000 were:

Security brokers and dealers: $66,000

Security and commodity services: $61,000

Commercial banks: $50,000

(Source: *Occupational Outlook Handbook, 2002–2003 Edition*)

## Duties and Responsibilities

A financial planner looks at a client's finances, determines how best to manage them, and helps the client achieve financial goals. Unlike stockbrokers or accountants, who concentrate on small, specific aspects of a person's finances, financial planners collaborate with their clients on the whole picture—where their money goes and why. Many financial planners work with the same client for years, helping them reach long- and short-term goals and revising plans as the economy shifts.

According to Kaplan Higher Education, most financial planners maintain a steady client base and consult by appointment only. Therefore, financial planners tend to set their own hours, work at their own pace, and consult in their office or travel to meet the clients where they live and work. Many planners even choose to open their own private practice: The BLS states that approximately 25 percent of all financial planners are self-employed, operating small investment advisory firms, usually located in urban areas.

## What You Need to Succeed

According to the BLS, a bachelor's degree in accounting, finance, economics, business, mathematics, or law provides good preparation for a position as a financial planner. Courses in investments, taxes, estate planning, and risk management also are helpful.

Certified Financial Planner™ (CFP™) is a certification granted by the Certified Financial Planner Board of Standards to those persons who complete an educational requirement and meet its ethics, experience, and examination requirements. Registered Financial Consultant (RFC) is a certification granted to individuals who successfully complete and maintain the seven qualification requirements (education, examination, ethics, experience, licensing, continued conduct, and continuing education) of the International Association of Registered Financial Consultants, Inc.

Strong interpersonal skills and sales ability are crucial to success. Mathematical, computer, analytical, and problem-solving skills are other essential qualities.

**ONLINE PROGRAM**

Kaplan College's online Certificate in Financial Planning provides the thorough educational foundation you need to enter this rapidly growing field. The program is designed to be completed within 18 months but may be completed more quickly depending on your professional and educational background. For more info, visit *www.kaplancollege.com*.

### The Inside Scoop

According to the BLS, financial planners who work for financial services firms are generally paid a salary plus bonus. Financial planners who are self-employed either charge hourly fees for their services or charge one set fee for a comprehensive plan based on its complexity. Financial planners who manage a client's assets usually charge a percentage of the assets.

### Career Ladder

Many financial planners enter the field after working in a related occupation, such as securities and financial services sales representative, insurance agent, accountant, or lawyer. Financial planners who work in firms may move into managerial positions, but most advance by accumulating clients and managing more assets.

## Insurance Underwriter

### Work Environment Wish List

Go back and check your Work Environment Wish List from the Introduction to this book. Did you rate any of the following characteristics as a "must have"? If so, you might be a good candidate for a job as an insurance underwriter.

- Clear-cut job description
- Desk job
- Regular hours
- Large company
- Training programs
- Job security
- Given responsibility and empowered to act
- Lots of time on a computer
- Work with customers, clients, vendors
- Predictable tasks each day/week/month
- Excellent job benefits

### Salary Range

Median annual earnings in the industries employing the largest number of insurance underwriters in 2000 were:

Fire, marine, and casualty insurance: $44,000

Life insurance: $43,000

Insurance agents, brokers, and service: $42,000

Medical service and health insurance: $38,000

(Source: *Occupational Outlook Handbook, 2002–2003 Edition*)

### Duties and Responsibilities

Insurance underwriters identify and calculate the risk of loss from policyholders, establish appropriate premium rates, and write policies that cover these risks.

According to the BLS, technology now plays an important role in an underwriter's job. Underwriters use computer applications called "smart systems" that automatically analyze and rate insurance applications, recommend acceptance or denial of the risk, and adjust the premium rate in accordance with the risk. Also, many insurance carriers' computer systems are now linked to different databases on the Internet that allow underwriters immediate access to information necessary in determining a potential client's risk.

### What You Need to Succeed

For entry-level underwriting jobs, most large insurance companies prefer college graduates who have a bachelor's degree in business administration or finance, with courses or experience in accounting.

If you're interested in a career as an insurance underwriter, you should be extremely analytical and detail-oriented. You also need to be a good decision-maker. Communication and interpersonal skills also are important, since much of the time you will be dealing with agents and other insurance professionals. Computer skills are essential, as well.

### The Inside Scoop

The BLS points out that there will always be a need for underwriters: It is a profession that is less subject to recession and layoffs than other fields because insurance is considered a necessity for people and businesses. However, it's a good idea to have a broad knowledge of insurance, so that you can transfer to another specialty if downsizing does occur.

### Career Ladder

New employees usually start as underwriter trainees or assistant underwriters. As trainees gain experience, they are assigned policy applications that are more complex and cover greater risks. Continuing education is a must: Experienced underwriters who complete courses of study may advance to senior underwriter or underwriting manager positions. Some underwriting managers are promoted to senior managerial jobs, although some employers require you to have a master's degree to reach this level.

## MARKETING CAREERS

### Advertising Account Executive

### Work Environment Wish List

Go back and check your Work Environment Wish List from the Introduction to this book. Did you rate any of the following characteristics as a "must have"? If so, you might be a good candidate for a job as an advertising account executive.

- Fast-paced
- Given responsibility and empowered to act
- Team player
- Opportunity to travel
- Work with customers, clients, vendors
- Creativity and initiative is rewarded
- Always something new
- Excellent job benefits

### Salary Range

Assistant account executive: $21,000–$30,000
Account executive: $30,000–$55,000

Account manager: $55,000–$100,000

(Source: *www.WetFeet.com*)

### Duties and Responsibilities

In advertising agencies, the majority of customer contact takes place through the account executive (AE). He or she works directly with clients, managing various aspects of their accounts. AEs ensure ongoing projects are running smoothly. They monitor the progress of the creative team, make sure deadlines are met, and answer any questions the client may have. Most are expected to find and pitch ideas to new prospects.

High earnings, substantial travel, and long hours—including evenings and weekends—are common.

### What You Need to Succeed

You should be mature, creative, highly motivated, resistant to stress, flexible, and decisive. The ability to communicate persuasively, both orally and in writing, with other managers, staff, and the public is vital. You also need tact, good judgment, and exceptional ability to establish and maintain effective personal relationships with supervisory and professional staff members and client firms.

Some employers look for a bachelor's degree in business administration, marketing, or journalism. A course of study should include marketing, consumer behavior, market research, sales, communication methods and technology, and visual arts. College graduates with related experience, a high level of creativity, and strong communication skills will have the best job opportunities.

### The Inside Scoop

According to *www.WetFeet.com*, few entry-level account management positions are advertised; most are filled by word of mouth. If you want to break into this field, you need to meet people already working in the industry. Proving yourself as an intern at an advertising agency is a great way to get hired as a full-time employee.

*Career Ladder*

To move up the career ladder, most people move from agency to agency in order to get to work on accounts for new clients. The entry-level position is usually an account coordinator or assistant account executive. The next step is account executive, and from there, you can become an account manager.

## Public Relations Specialist

*Work Environment Wish List*

Go back and check your Work Environment Wish List from the Introduction to this book. Did you rate any of the following characteristics as a "must have"? If so, you might be a good candidate for a job as a public relations specialist.

- Fast paced
- Large company
- Periodic evaluations with chance for advancement
- Given responsibility and empowered to act
- Team player
- Opportunity to travel
- Work with customers, clients, vendors
- Creativity and initiative is rewarded
- Always something new
- Periodic job evaluations tied to merit increases in pay
- Fast lane open for advancement
- Excellent job benefits

*Salary Range*

Entry-level: $20,000–$30,000

Public relations specialist: $30,000–$54,000

Senior PR manager: $75,000–$150,000

(Source: *www.WetFeet.com* and *Occupational Outlook Handbook, 2002–2003 Edition*)

## Duties and Responsibilities

Public relations specialists serve as advocates for businesses, nonprofit associations, universities, hospitals, and other organizations, and build and maintain positive relationships with the public.

An important part of a public relations specialist's job is to inform the general public, interest groups, and stockholders of an organization's policies, activities, and accomplishments. Public relations specialists also get to prepare press releases and contact the media to try to convince them to print or broadcast their material.

## What You Need to Succeed

The BLS states that opportunities should be best for college graduates who combine a degree in public relations or other communications-related fields with a public relations internship or other related work experience.

To be a public relations specialist, you need an outgoing personality, self-confidence, an understanding of human psychology, and an enthusiasm for motivating people. You should be flexible, competitive, and able to function as part of a team. The ability to write and speak well is absolutely essential.

## The Inside Scoop

If you're looking for a 9-to-5 job, public relations might not be for you: Unpaid overtime is common, and occasionally, you might be asked to be at the office or on call around the clock—especially if there is an emergency or crisis.

## Career Ladder

If you pursue a career in corporate public relations, you may be hired by a large company's communications department as a PR coordinator, doing administrative projects such as clipping newspapers, assisting in research, maintaining a list of media contacts, and coordinating mailings of press packets to the media. The next step is becoming a PR specialist, and then a PR manager. From there, it's possible to become a vice president or senior vice president of communications. Another option is to strike out on your own and become a PR consultant.

If you pursue a career track in a public relations firm, you might be hired as an account coordinator or account assistant, and then be promoted to account executive, account manager, and possibly even director.


# MANAGEMENT CAREERS

## Store Manager

### *Work Environment Wish List*

Go back and check your Work Environment Wish List from the Introduction to this book. Did you rate any of the following characteristics as a "must have"? If so, you might be a good candidate for a job as a store manager.

- Clear-cut job description
- Closely knit employee group
- Training programs
- Job security
- Work with customers, clients, vendors
- Train others
- Predictable tasks each day/week/month
- Periodic job evaluations tied to merit increases in pay

### *Salary Range*

Median annual earnings for salaried store managers in these industries in 2000 were:

Grocery stores: $27,000

Department stores: $24,000

(Source: *Occupational Outlook Handbook, 2002–2003 Edition*)

### *Duties and Responsibilities*

If you follow a career in retailing and manage a small boutique, you'll probably hire staff, select and buy merchandise, oversee advertising (radio and print), assist customers, and even plan the budget and manage accounting.

In large retail establishments, you'll provide day-to-day oversight of an individual department. Your area of responsibility is likely to be limited. You may supervise the sales force and be responsible for inventory, especially as it relates to seasonal cycles. (It's not acceptable to take up floor space with lots of winter goods when it's summertime!)

Most store managers work 40 hours or more a week. Long hours are common during sales events and holidays. They are expected to work evenings and weekends, but usually are compensated with a day off during the week.

### What You Need to Succeed

College graduates usually can enter management training programs directly. Recommended courses include accounting, marketing, management, and sales, as well as psychology, sociology, and communication. Store managers today must also be computer literate, because almost all cash registers and inventory control systems are computerized.

Important qualities include leadership, team-building skills, self confidence, motivation, and decisiveness.

### The Inside Scoop

No matter whether you want to be the store manager in a large department store or a small boutique or retail shop, you're more likely to get a job offer if you already have retail job experience. Taking a part-time job in a retail setting while you're working to earn your degree in business administration prepares you to get your foot in the door.

### Career Ladder

Many national retail chains and companies have formal training programs for management trainees that include both classroom and onsite training. If you're employed at a large department store, you'll probably be hired in a management trainee position and work as an assistant manager for at least one year. An assistant store manager earns hourly wages; the store manager earns an annual salary and bonus dollars related to sales performance at his or her store. Large establishments often have extensive career ladder programs, and may offer managers the opportunity to transfer to another store in the chain or to the central office if an opening occurs. Some managers who have worked in their industry for a long time open their own stores.

## City Manager

### *Work Environment Wish List*

Go back and check your Work Environment Wish List from the Introduction to this book. Did you rate any of the following characteristics as a "must have"? If so, you might be a good candidate for a job as a city manager.

- Clear-cut job description
- Fast paced
- Given responsibility and empowered to act
- Team player
- Convenient work location
- Work with customers, clients, vendors
- Meaningful work

### *Salary Range*

According to the International City/County Management Association (ICMA), the median annual salaries for these local government employees in 2000 were:

City manager: $75,000

Assistant chief administrative officer: $60,000

Economic development/planning director: $58,000

(Source: *Occupational Outlook Handbook, 2002–2003 Edition*)

### *Duties and Responsibilities*

In 1908 in Staunton, Virginia, the first city manager was appointed, marking the birth of a new career. Today, approximately 3,000 local governments in the United States operate with a council-manager plan; each one engages a city manager. The International City/County Management Association (ICMA) website (*www.icma.org*) explains this concept: "Under the council-manager form, power is concentrated in the elected council, which hires a professional administrator to implement its policies. This appointee serves at the pleasure of the council and has responsibility for preparing the budget, directing day-to-day operations, hiring and firing personnel, and serving as the council's chief policy advisor."

According to the Texas City Management Association (TCMA) website (*www.tcma.org*), "The council-manager form of government is widely used in the United States. It has proven to be successful in large part because it stresses professionalism in city government." There's no reason to believe this won't continue.

Some of the things a city manager does:

- Operates according to the city charter
- Works with elected officials
- Manages a large staff of employees
- Prepares and submits an annual budget estimate to the council

### What You Need to Succeed

The BLS states that city managers have major responsibilities and must bring many skills and years of experience to the job. A master's degree in public administration is widely recommended, but not required, for city managers.

To be a city manager, you should be flexible, detail-oriented, and able to reconcile different viewpoints. The ability to communicate effectively, both orally and in writing, is essential for anyone interested in this field.

### The Inside Scoop

It's not realistic to think that as soon as you have your associate's or bachelor's degree in business administration, you're ready to apply for a job as a city manager. Nevertheless, there's no time like the present to become aware of this position. How else can you know if you'd like to go for it? As a matter of fact, while you're in high school or upon graduation you might find a part time or entry-level job in a city manager's office. If you discover that you like what you find, you'll be gaining experience that moves you along this career path.

### Career Ladder

City managers may start out as management analysts or assistants in government departments working with councils and mayors. After several years, they may be hired to manage a town or a small city and eventually become manager of larger cities.

## Human Resources Specialist

### Work Environment Wish List

Go back and check your Work Environment Wish List from the Introduction to this book. Did you rate any of the following characteristics as a "must have"? If so, you might be a good candidate for a job as a human resources specialist.

- Clear-cut job description
- Large company
- Regular hours
- Training programs
- Periodic evaluations with chance for advancement
- Job security
- Team player
- Lots of time on a computer
- Work with customers, clients, vendors
- Train others
- Periodic job evaluations tied to merit increases in pay
- Excellent job benefits

### Salary Range

According to a 2001 survey of compensation in the human resources field, conducted by Abbott, Langer, and Associates of Crete, Illinois, the median total cash compensation for selected personnel and labor relations occupations were:

Human resources records specialist: $33,000

Job evaluation specialist: $43,000

Benefits supervisor: $60,000

Recruitment and interviewing manager: $70,000

Compensation manager: $80,000

(Source: *Occupational Outlook Handbook, 2002–2003 Edition*)

### Duties and Responsibilities

Human resources specialists help establish and maintain the relationship between employer and employee. They also help their company to use employee skills effectively, provide training opportunities to enhance those skills, and boost employee satisfaction with their jobs and working conditions.

In a large organization, human resources staff members will specialize in a specific area. Employment or recruitment specialists screen, interview, and sometimes test applicants; they also may check references and extend job offers. Compensation specialists devise ways to ensure fair and equitable pay rates. Benefits specialists handle a company's employee benefits program, notably its health insurance and pension plans. In a small organization, a human resources generalist may handle all aspects of human resources work, requiring a broad range of knowledge.

### What You Need to Succeed

Employers generally seek college graduates for entry-level human resources jobs. A combination of courses in business administration, social sciences, and behavioral sciences is a useful background for human resources. Knowledge of computers and information systems is also useful.

You cannot have a career in human resources unless you're able to speak and write effectively. Open-mindedness is another important quality; after all, you'll be working with or supervising people with different cultural backgrounds, levels of education, and experience. You must be able to cope with conflicting points of view and demonstrate discretion, integrity, and a congenial personality.

### The Inside Scoop

According to the BLS, an advanced degree is becoming increasingly important for some human resources positions. For instance, a background in law is useful for employee benefits managers and others who must interpret the growing number of laws and regulations. A master's degree in business administration with a concentration in human resources management is a good idea for those seeking top HR management positions.

*Career Ladder*

Entry-level employees in human resources commonly start out by performing administrative duties. You might enter formal or on-the-job training programs in which you'll learn how to classify jobs, interview applicants, or administer employee benefits. You will then be assigned to specific areas in the human resources department to gain experience. Later, you may advance to a managerial position, overseeing a major element of the personnel program-compensation or training, for example. Exceptional human resources workers may be promoted to director of personnel or industrial relations, which can eventually lead to a top managerial or executive position.

# Chapter Four

# PREPARING FOR YOUR CAREER

You probably know more about preparation than you think you know, because you've been doing it all your life. Did you:

- Practice riding a bicycle before you became a competent rider?
- Study multiplication tables until you were able to come up with the answers quickly?
- Try out for the softball team before you became a team member?
- Obtain a learner's permit before you got your driver's license?
- It's easy to build a long list of accomplishments that came about as a result of preparation. Preparing for your career is no different.

You're aware of what you like and what you don't like, or that some things are easy for you to do and some things aren't easy. Life experiences have helped you to gain insights, and what you've learned is of terrific value to you now. The fact that you're reading this book, which delivers targeted career information, confirms you know how to go about getting what you want!

**YOUR CAREER GOALS**

Most jobs have certain educational requirements. It's a good idea to keep your career goals in mind when deciding what kind of education you're going to pursue.

## EDUCATIONAL REQUIREMENTS

The easiest way to discover what's required in earning a degree in business administration is to obtain that information from colleges that offer the program. Not only will you want to know what courses you will need to satisfy degree requirements, you'll want to know whether you're well prepared to succeed. If you feel you're not prepared, there's plenty you can do to remedy the situation right now!

*Illustration:* A sample first-semester schedule at the University of Arizona's Eller College of Business and Public Administration is as follows:

| | |
|---|---|
| Freshman Composition | 3 units |
| Introduction to Computers | 3 units |
| Business Administration 101 | 1 unit |
| General Education | <u>6 units</u> |
| TOTAL | 13 units |

Katie is about to enter her senior year of high school. She reviews the list of elective courses available to her in high school (i.e., music, art, writing) and chooses to take a class in creative writing. She reasons, "Since I'll need to take 3 units of Freshman Composition if I go to Eller College of Business, I'd better take this class now to sharpen my writing skills."

*Illustration:* Ken has never been a good student. He finds himself about to begin his senior year of high school and realizes he wants to earn a good living. He equates this goal with attending college. His high school guidance counselor speaks with him about earning a degree in business administration, and Ken is enthusiastic about the prospect. However, his counselor reminds him, "Your high school grades have been very low. You've got a lot of catching up to do."

In the past, Ken had often skipped going to class and his homework assignments were usually incomplete. Now, all that changed. A few weeks later, when Ken's guidance counselor hands him a Recommended Reading List, Ken says, "I've read most of these books."

His guidance counselor is delighted. "You're going to do fine, Ken. Just remember, you don't have any room to slip backward into old ways. If your work and study habits continue to be excellent and you continue to read so many fine books, you should do well in college. The bad news is you may not be accepted at the college of your choice.

The good news is you can probably attend the local community college, get top grades, and eventually transfer to a college that's more of a challenge to you."

# TWO- OR FOUR-YEAR COLLEGES

## Weighing Your Degree Options

As we've discussed, it's possible to get a degree in business administration by attending a two-year or four-year college. Obviously, you'll narrow college selections to those institutions that offer the degree you want. College location, tuition costs, and campus size are some of the other factors that you'll need to consider.

The following questions and answers are designed to help you weigh the merits of a two-year program vs. a four-year program. (This kind of evaluation is different from deciding if a campus is too big or small, if extra curricular opportunities suit you, etc.) Only you can decide which is the best option for you.

> **WHY DO I NEED A DEGREE?**
>
> A degree is proof that you've completed the required education for the subject. It implies that you have the required skills needed to do the job for which you are applying.

**Q. Is it less expensive to attend a two-year college?**

**A.** In the short run, yes. You'll spend less time pursuing your degree, so you'll have to pay for two instead of four years' worth of tuition, books, fees, etc. Also, when you're in school, you're not generating the income you can expect from full-time employment; theoretically, you'll have two more years of earned income in your lifetime by attending a two-year school vs. a four-year program.

However, in the long run, a bachelor's degree will open more doors for you and lead to higher-paying jobs. In other words, if we look at paying for your education as an investment in your future, a bachelor's degree will give you a greater return on your investment.

**Q. Will an associate's degree open doors for me in the workplace?**

**A.** Of course. If this weren't so, the two-year program wouldn't have been created. All accredited institutions of learning meet certain standards, which are generally viewed as highly desirable. Make sure a well-respected group accredits the college you attend. Many community colleges are supported by and praised by local employers. If you plan to settle in the area once you earn your degree, you may want to participate in internships or summer programs the local employers develop in cooperation with the junior college. This employment can lead to full employment after graduation.

However, keep in mind that you may not be eligible for certain entry-level jobs without a bachelor's degree.

**Q. After earning an associate's degree, can I return to school to earn a bachelor's degree after I've worked for a few years?**

**A.** It's possible, but you may have to satisfy special requirements such as returning to the classroom within a short period of time or risk forfeiting the value of some already earned college credits. If you are considering this possibility, talk with the admissions counselors at a four-year college and get specific information. You should also speak with people who have done this or are doing it. Some people find it difficult to return to the classroom after being in the workplace full-time. Other people find that their work experience makes it easier to do well in the classroom.

**Q. Will the two-year college have good research facilities?**

**A.** This question has no one-size-fits-all answer. Check with a specific college admission's office personnel to get answers. A junior college may be affiliated with a larger library at a nearby university so their students have library privileges in both places. But generally speaking, today's libraries are not judged so much by the number of books on the shelves, the square feet devoted to the library, or the research staff available to assist students. Computer access to the Internet has opened new avenues to obtain information and to conduct do-it-yourself research. Investing in a desktop or laptop computer is a wise decision for any student.

## Finding the Right College

Once you decide what type of degree you want to earn, it's time to start looking for a college! Here are some guidelines for evaluating colleges:

- Visit the school with someone you trust—a parent, spouse, friend, etc. That way, you'll have another person with whom to compare notes.
- Write down your questions and concerns, such as those listed below. Have them with you when you visit or call.
    - Is the program accredited?
    - Does the admissions staff take time to talk with you? Do they answer your questions or get back to you when they find the answers?

- Is financial aid available?
- What are the instructors' academic qualifications? How much practical experience do they have in the subject they teach?
- Is the school accessible by public transportation? (That might not seem like an issue now, but it could be a big one if you have an unreliable car or a young child to take to school each day.)
- What's your overall impression? Do you feel welcome? Do the classrooms look like places where you'd be comfortable? Is the equipment up-to-date? Do the students appear interested and involved in what's going on? Are the teachers knowledgeable, friendly, confident, and receptive to questions?
- What are the job placement rates?
- Request the names, numbers or email addresses of recent graduates. Contact them and ask the questions on the "Discussion Points with Recent Grads" sheet on page 62. This input will be especially valuable if you're considering an out-of-town school.

Do not expect any one school to have all the attributes you are looking for. Just as in life, you have to weigh the good with the bad and decide which is best for your situation. You must evaluate the answers and pick the school that best meets your needs.

## COLLEGE FACT SHEET

The sheet below will help you organize and compare findings from your school visits. Make photocopies of this page or put the information on the computer so you'll have one sheet for each facility you visit.

**Date:** _______________________________________________

**School or training program:** _______________________________

    Phone _______________________________________________

    Address_______________________________________________

    Website _______________________________________________

**Admissions director or contact person:** _______________________

    Phone _______________________________________________

    Fax _______________________________________________

    Email _______________________________________________

**Department head:** _______________________________________

    Phone _______________________________________________

    Email _______________________________________________

**Career Services director:** _________________________________

    Phone _______________________________________________

    Email _______________________________________________

**Job placement rates:** _____________________________________

**Tuition:** _______________________________________________

    Extra fees: Parking, lab supplies, etc. ___________________________

    Books _______________________________________________

**Application deadline:** _____________________________________

**Application fee:** _________________________________________

**Length of training:** _______________________________________________

**Prerequisites:** __________________________________________________

**Certificate or degree awarded:** ___________________________________

**Size of classes:**_________________________________________________

    Student-to-teacher ratios (lectures/labs/field training)_____________________

**Schedule:** _____________________________________________________

    First day of class_______________________________________________

    Class hours _________________________________________________

    Graduation date_______________________________________________

**Recent graduates:** ______________________________________________

    1. Name ____________________________________________________

    Phone/Email_________________________________________________

    2. Name ____________________________________________________

    Phone/Email_________________________________________________

**Overall impressions:** ____________________________________________

    Your impressions______________________________________________

    Your companion's impressions ___________________________________

**Follow-up questions for staff:** ___________________________________

    1. ________________________________________________________

    2. ________________________________________________________

    3. ________________________________________________________

## DISCUSSION POINTS WITH RECENT GRADS

**Name:** _______________________________________________

Phone _________________________________________________

Email __________________________________________________

**Date of conversation:** ________________________________

1. In general, did you get your money's worth from the training?___________

   _____________________________________________________

2. Would you recommend the program to other students? ___________

   _____________________________________________________

3. How much time did you spend studying? Do you think that was more, less, or about the same as other students?___________________________

   _____________________________________________________

4. Were the instructors helpful?________________________________

   _____________________________________________________

5. Is it easy for students to get extra help if they need it? Is there an extra fee?

   _____________________________________________________

6. What were the exams like?

   _____________________________________________________

7. How much assistance did the Career Services department give with interviews and job placements?________________________________

   _____________________________________________________

8. If you had it to do over again, would you sign up for the same certificate or degree? ______________________________________________

   _____________________________________________________

9. What is the school's reputation among employers? ___________

   _____________________________________________________

10. May I call you if I have more questions? ___________________

   _____________________________________________________

# DISTANCE LEARNING

Today, education is not bound by time or place. The path to earning a degree can take many routes, depending upon your individual circumstances and needs. Distance learning has created a whole new way to earn a degree. Courses can be taken at your own pace and fit into your own schedule, so that you're free to work or study during the day or night as you see fit.

Distance learning programs make it possible for you to get a degree without stepping inside a college building. Typically all study and interactive communication is accomplished electronically. In other words, you'll use your computer to communicate with professors, instructors, and other students in order to earn your degree.

There are now more than 2,000 institutions, some with the highest academic credentials, that offer online courses and degrees accessible from anywhere with a computer and a modem. The size and scope of the many institutions vary from small to large, with the largest signing up students for as many as 44,000 courses in one year. It has become a multibillion dollar market worldwide. Some institutions are "virtual," existing only in cyberspace, while others are "normal" colleges and universities that offer online courses in addition to their regular classroom-based programs.

But is online education equivalent to the traditional bricks-and-mortar school? And, more importantly, will employers value degrees earned online? Actually, a number of recent studies indicate that outcomes for students in distance learning programs can be equal to or better than the results achieved by students in traditional classes. In one study, Arizona State University compared test results of its online M.B.A. students with those enrolled in the traditional program and found that their online students scored higher.

As for the second question of whether employers accept or support distance education, it should be noted that many business leaders participate in devel-

**ONLINE DEGREE DIRECTORY**

To learn more about institutions offering business degree programs online, visit *www.worldwidelearn.com/business-degrees.htm*.

**GET YOUR CERTIFICATE**

A student must complete the following online courses to earn a Certificate in Accounting and Finance from Kaplan College:

| Course Title | Credits |
| --- | --- |
| Accounting I | 4 |
| Spreadsheet Applications | 4 |
| Statistics | 4 |
| Accounting II | 4 |
| Finance | 4 |
| Business Law | 4 |
| Managerial Finance and Accounting | 6 |
| Management of Information Systems | 6 |
| **TOTAL** | **36** |

oping programs that anticipate workplace needs. Also, a number of distance learning institutions employ executive and senior-level professionals as faculty, enabling students to gain from the experience and real-world insights of the instructors.

### Is Distance Learning Right for Me?

The concept of distance education may appeal to you, but are you the kind of person who should do it? The following attributes are ones you need to consider:

- You'll need to be a self-starter, someone who is disciplined and will get online and attend classes and complete assignments in a timely fashion. If you're the type of person who needs close supervision to keep you on track, you'll probably become frustrated and not want to continue.
- Do you have other responsibilities to handle while obtaining a degree? Perhaps you provide care for a young child or hold a full-time job. Although you will need some uninterrupted time to devote to your studies, flexibility is perhaps the biggest benefit of distance learning.
- Students who are physically challenged may be especially attracted to the ease of virtually staying in one place and attending school online.

## THE APPLICATION AND ADMISSION PROCESS

This is an exciting time in your life. At the same time, it's possible to encounter *information overload*. Take a deep breath. The admission process is a matter of following instructions: Find out what's required, and follow through.

Interestingly, the application process is pretty much the same for most two-year, four-year, and distance learning institutions. Many schools have application deadlines each year. However, many schools accept applications on a "rolling" basis. Keep in mind that some programs fill up fast; in general, the earlier you apply, the better.

Most schools post their admissions requirements on their website or will mail them to you if you request an information packet or admissions application. If you have all your materials together, admission can be quick and painless. Here are the basics:

- An official high school transcript; a GED (General Education Development) certificate may also be acceptable

- Completed application form
- Letters of recommendation from your teachers, guidance counselor, employer, or someone else in a position to evaluate your abilities
- Standardized test scores, such as SAT I, ACT, or SAT II test scores
- FAFSA or other financial aid forms (see chapter 5 for more information on financial aid)

Review the application form carefully, and don't hesitate to ask the admissions staff for assistance. In fact, they'll probably offer to walk you through it.

## Your High School Transcript

The kinds of classes you take during your high school years deliver an important message. A college admissions officer wants to admit students who are likely to succeed. Good grades earned in less challenging elective courses will be noticed. A good grade in a typing class probably doesn't rate as high as a good grade in a biology class. This isn't to suggest that typing isn't important; good typing skills can be a major time-saver during your college years. Still, your transcript should show you did well in the more difficult college prep classes. It's then assumed you are able to grasp complex data, read extensively, write acceptable reports, participate in classroom discussions, have good study habits, and pass difficult exams.

Your high school transcript will be sent to colleges of your choice before you earn your diploma. In most cases, college admissions personnel will want to see the "finished product," too. The end of your senior year is not a time to rest. "When I rest, I rust," is an old saying. Rusting is not an option here!

---

**COURSES OF ONLINE STUDY**

Kaplan College offers the following online business degrees and certifications:

- Bachelor of Science Degree in Management/Applied Management
- Bachelor of Science Degree in Management/Information Technology Management
- Associate of Science Degree in Applied Management
- Associate of Science Degree in Interdisciplinary Studies
- 2 + 2 Bachelor's Degree Completion Programs
- Financial Planning Certificate
- Accounting and Finance Certificate
- E-Commerce Certificate
- Health Care Management Certificate
- Sales and Marketing Certificate

*Kaplan College is accredited by the Commission on Institutions of Higher Education of the North Central Association of Colleges and Schools (NCA).*

## Letters of Recommendation

Letters of recommendation may be mentioned in passing, but in fact, when they're well done they can catapult you into an enviable position.

You're in the driver's seat when it comes to deciding whom to ask for a letter. You may have always earned high grades in your English classes, but that doesn't mean your English teacher is necessarily the best person to write your letter. The writer should be enthusiastic and a good salesperson. The letter of recommendation must sell you to the admissions staff! How about your part-time employer? Or, perhaps a ballet teacher or a scout leader knows you well and would be flattered to be asked to do this for you. When a person who knows you well writes a letter of recommendation, that person is able to "write with heart." He or she doesn't have to search for something to say, because the relationship you established gives the recommender something "real" to write about.

When you ask someone for a recommendation, permit the person to politely decline. ("Would you feel comfortable about writing a letter of recommendation for me?" or "Do you have time to write an important letter for me?") Listen carefully to the response you receive. If the person hesitates, you may prefer to ask someone else.

Think about how the letter looks—not merely what it says. If, for example, it's prepared on fine stationery, is typewritten or computer generated, and has ample margins, it looks good to the reader. Of course, there shouldn't be spelling errors or erasures. How can you control this if you don't write the letter? You control whom you ask to write the letter and it all begins there. But, you may specify that you would appreciate it if the writer uses stationery with the company letterhead or that the writer doesn't handwrite the letter. If you offer reasonable explanations for your requests (e.g., "I understand college admissions people prefer typewritten letters"), the writer is likely to comply without giving your request a second thought.

# MAKE THE MOST OF COLLEGE

If there was one common theme we heard from recent graduates, it was this: Put your heart and soul into your training! If you show your commitment from day one, your instructors and the career services staff will be eager to match you up with the best employers.

Grades count, but there's more to it. Your instructors will also expect punctuality, attendance, and reliability. If you have to miss a day, ask the teacher how you can catch up. If you have problems with a subject, arrange for extra help before you get in over your head.

## Office of Career Services

The career services staff connects the school to the job market. They're always in touch with employers, scouting out possibilities for internships, co-ops, and entry-level work. Thanks to the efforts of the career services staff, many students have jobs in place even before they graduate.

The role of the Office of Career Services specifically includes:

- Assisting with internships
- Posting information about career fairs
- Providing tips on "working" the career fairs (employers to visit, questions to ask)
- Teaching job search skills including, cover letter, résumé and interview techniques
- Coaching on appropriate dress and professional conduct
- Writing letters of reference
- Finding and sharing job leads
- Follow-up throughout internships and first jobs to ensure a good fit for student and employer
- Lifetime career assistance

# CERTIFICATION REQUIREMENTS

What is **certification**? The procedure through which an official designation is obtained; often involves standardized testing. (This definition was obtained from *www.investorwords.com*.)

In addition to on-the-job learning after you obtain your degree in business administration, you may decide to prepare for special examinations that lead to certification. Various certifications are awarded by different organizations. In many cases, a certification announces that you're especially good at what you do. Employers often reward this achievement with higher wages. Check with people who have earned certifications to learn more. Don't forget to ask about costs associated with certification.

Illustration: When Jack completed two years of study for his business administration degree, he was hired for part-time work at a local stock brokerage office. His supervisor was Nancy James, CFA. Jack learned that *CFA* referred to *Chartered Financial Analyst.*

"What tests did you take to earn this certification?" Jack asked. "Do you think this is something I should consider pursuing?"

Ms. James explained, "A CFA must pass three levels of tests in economics, accounting, security analysis, and money management. The tests are administered by the Association for Investment Management and Research (AIMR). If you're serious about a career as an investment analyst, portfolio manager, high–net-worth money manager, credit analyst, or any career that deals primarily with the investment decision-making process, you should definitely consider getting this certification."

> **DID YOU KNOW?**
>
> The global median income of an AIMR member with more than 10 years of experience is well over $200,000. Visit *www.aimr.org* to download informational pamphlets and learn more about the specifics of the CFA Program.

She went on to tell Jack that some people in the industry obtain other types of certification, such as *RIA (Registered Investment Advisor)*, *CFC (Chartered Financial Consultant)*, and one that was familiar to Jack, *CPA (Certified Public Accountant).*

Jack thought about his cousin, who recently earned her certification to teach school in New Jersey. She was excited when the actual paper certification arrived in the mail. "This makes it official," she said. "This tells everyone that I've done everything necessary to be a bona fide teacher in New Jersey."

Now Jack understands exactly what she means. He was a long way from being able to pass special tests in economics, accounting, and security analysis and money management. But he recognized that anyone with certification in a field is likely to be highly skilled at their job and respected in their field.

## Points to Consider

- It's useful to know that certification possibilities exist. In terms of career enhancement, consider this: You may enjoy higher earnings than people doing the same job who don't have certification.

- You may be forced to participate in continuing education classes in order to maintain a certification. Instead of relying upon good intentions to stay up to date, this requirement guarantees that you'll stay on the cutting-edge of your career.

- Certification is not available in every field of work. And, in some fields of work, certification may be highly prized while in others it may be "no big deal."

# PAYING FOR YOUR EDUCATION

Paying for your education may be the single most difficult challenge you will face in the next few years. The ideal way to pay for school is to write a check up front. But with current costs running anywhere from $2,000 to $100,000, few of us have the means. Before we get sidetracked on the high cost of getting an education, however, let's discuss the cost of not getting an education.

According to the latest U.S. Census Bureau figures, the median annual income for workers age 25 and over with:

- A high school diploma is $27,150
- Some college training, no degree is $32,200
- An associate's degree is $35,100
- A bachelor's degree is $44,000

But the money is just one piece of it. You probably know this if you've ever talked with someone who's 40-something and still wishes he or she had gone on to school. That regret is another cost of not getting an education.

Unless you can earn a handsome salary, it probably doesn't pay to postpone your education while you save for tuition. If you earn minimum wage, as most high-school graduates do, you're better off to start school

### PAY AS YOU GO

One option is to work as you learn and graduate debt-free. With night classes and a day job, or vice versa, some people do manage it. That may be practical if:

- Your income is high enough to cover your living expenses and educational costs.
- You can arrange your schedule to manage classroom, homework, and personal obligations.

and take out loans. After you have your certification or degree, you'll earn two or three times minimum wage and you can pay back the loans in much less time than you could save in advance.

If financial aid seems a wise choice, the tools below will help you figure out how much to borrow.

## ESTIMATE YOUR LIVING EXPENSES

One way to calculate your daily expenses is to record every single expenditure over three months. If you choose that method, it will mean carrying a pocket notebook and writing down every penny you spend and what it's spent for. Be sure to add in periodic expenses like auto insurance, license plates or registration fees, and health insurance and copayments.

Another way to nail down your living expenses is to fill out a budget sheet such as the "Personal Expense Estimates" sheet below. This picture of your spending habits might help you tighten the budget for school. For example, could you pack your lunch instead of visiting the vending machine? Could you tape programs on TV instead of renting movies? The blunt truth is, your "entertainment" might come down to an extra hour of sleep, especially in a full-time degree program!

### PERSONAL EXPENSE ESTIMATES

Skipping the items that don't apply to you, sort the "yearly expenses" column into what you'll have to spend during training. Those numbers will plug into your estimated educational expense table.

| Expense | Monthly | Yearly |
| --- | --- | --- |
| Housing | | |
| Rent or house payment | | |
| Electricity | | |
| Heat & air conditioning | | |
| Water bill | | |
| Trash pick-up | | |

| | | |
|---|---|---|
| Phone and long distance | | |
|     Internet connection | | |
|     Cable service | | |
| Transportation* | | |
|     Car payment | | |
|     Auto insurance | | |
|     License or registration fee | | |
|     Repairs | | |
|     Gas | | |
|     Bus fare | | |
|     Parking | | |
| Food | | |
|     Groceries | | |
|     Restaurant meals & snacks | | |
| Health insurance | | |
|     Monthly premiums | | |
|     Co-pays | | |
|     Prescriptions & over-the-counter drugs | | |
| Other insurance | | |
|     Renter's | | |
|     Life | | |
|     Other | | |
| Dependent care | | |
|     Child care | | |
|     Child support | | |
|     Alimony | | |
|     Other | | |
| Credit card payment | | |
| Clothing | | |
|     Self | | |
|     Dependent(s) | | |

| | | |
|---|---|---|
| Personal care services & products | | |
| Self | | |
| Dependent(s) | | |
| Entertainment | | |
| Other expenses | | |
|    1. | | |
|    2. | | |
|    3. | | |

*If you move away for training, your transportation costs may include occasional visits back home.

If you'd rather computerize your expense records, try one of the personal finance packages from a software store for around $25, or go to *www.personalbudgeting.com* for a sample budget.

## ESTIMATE YOUR EDUCATIONAL EXPENSES

You'll hear the term *Cost of Attendance* in connection with student loans. Here's the definition: The estimated total amount it will cost to go to school. It's usually expressed as a yearly figure including:

| Expense | Yearly Amount |
|---|---|
| Tuition and fees | |
| Living Expenses (from above) | |
| Books | |
| Supplies | |
| Transportation | |
| Loan fees | |
| Miscellaneous expenses such as rental or purchase of a computer | |
| **Total** | |

# ESTIMATE YOUR INCOME

Fill in the amounts you expect to receive while you are in school.

| Expected Income | Monthly | Yearly |
|---|---|---|
| Personal earnings (take home) | | |
| Savings or investment income | | |
| Family contribution (spouse, parents, grandparents, etc.) | | |
| Child support | | |
| Alimony | | |
| Aid to Families with Dependent Children (AFDC) | | |
| Veterans benefits | | |
| Social Security | | |

# HOW MUCH FINANCIAL AID WILL YOU NEED?

If your expected income is less than your cost of living and educational expenses, financial aid is your best alternative.

The amount of student financial aid (SFA) for which you may qualify is based on the U.S. Department of Education's financial need formula:

Cost of Attendance

– Expected Family Contribution

= Financial need

The financial aid administrator at the school will put together a financial aid package that comes as close as possible to your need. But federal funds are limited, so you may receive less than your official "financial need." The "SFA Thumbnail Sketch" below gives you an overview of federal assistance.

> **EXPECTED FAMILY CONTRIBUTION (EFC)**
>
> The formula used to calculate your EFC is established by law and is used to measure your family's financial strength on the basis of your family's income and assets.

# STUDENT FINANCIAL AID (SFA): THUMBNAIL SKETCH

There are three types of federal financial assistance. While the majority of accredited technical schools and colleges offer financial aid, they don't necessarily have all the programs.

- A *grant* is money that does not have to be repaid. The amount of a grant is based on need, training costs and enrollment status.
- A *loan* is money that must be repaid with interest. Loans are made to students or parents paying for a child's schooling.
- *Work-study* is money for education paid by the school for on-campus or community-based work.

## GOING FOR GRANTS

- Pell Grants for the 2002–2003 school year ranged from $400 to $4,000 per school year.
- Federal Supplemental Educational Opportunity Grants ranged from $100 to $4,000.

## Who Gets SFA?

To be eligible for financial aid, you must:

- Be a U.S. citizen or eligible noncitizen of the United States with a valid social security number
- Have a high school diploma, General Education Development (GED) certificate, or pass a federally approved "ability to benefit" test
- Enroll in an eligible program as a regular degree or certificate student
- Register (or have registered) for selective service (the military), if you are a male between ages 18 and 25

Most students who are entering college or a career school straight from high school are considered *dependent* students. If you are dependent, you have to report both your and your parents' financial information. This information will be considered when your eligibility is determined.

If you're an *independent* student, you'll need to report only your own income and assets (and those of your spouse, if you're married). For the 2002–2003 academic year, you're an independent student if at least one of the following applies to you:

- You were born before January 1, 1979.
- You're married.

- You are or will be enrolled in a master's or doctoral program (beyond a bachelor's degree) during the 2002–2003 school year.
- You have children who receive more than half their support from you.
- You have dependents (other than your children or spouse) who live with you and who receive more than half of their support from you and will continue to receive more than half their support from you through June 30, 2003.
- You're an orphan or ward of the court (or were a ward of the court until age 18).
- You're a veteran of the U.S. Armed Forces.

## How Do You Get SFA?

Application for federal student assistance is free. Some institutions do charge an application fee for institutional grants or scholarships.

> **APPLYING ONLINE**
>
> *FAFSA on the Web* is an interactive webpage where you can complete and submit your FAFSA over the Internet. Visit *www.fafsa.ed.gov* to get started.

1. Complete the Free Application for Federal Student Aid (FAFSA). Start early—as soon as you decide to apply to a training program. Copies of the form are available through your high school guidance office, college, or career school financial aid office, public libraries, the Federal Student Aid Information Center at 1-800-433-3243, or online at *www.fafsa.ed.gov*.

   Your eligibility is determined one award year at a time. Because your circumstances can change greatly from one year to the next, you must complete an application each award year. After you've applied for the first time, you might be able to apply easier and faster in subsequent award years by completing a Renewal FAFSA. With a Renewal FAFSA, you have to fill out only the information that changed from the previous award year.

2. If you submit the FAFSA on your own, you'll receive a Student Aid Report (SAR) within one to four weeks, listing your Expected Family Contribution (the amount you and your family are expected to contribute toward your education). That amount may not match what you and your family end up contributing. If you submit the FAFSA through the school, they will tell you how much aid they can offer.

## FINANCIAL AID APPLICATION CHECKLIST

Before you sit down to complete the FAFSA, gather up the necessary paperwork. Actually, says Elaine Neely-Eacona of Quest Education, "filling out an application is much like filing an income tax return." At career and technical schools, "students typically start classes in January, so use that year's tax return even if you haven't filed it yet," she suggests. (For a January 2003 enrollment, use your 2002 tax return.)

- Driver's license
- Social Security card
- W-2 Forms (tax documents from employers stating wages paid during the year) and records of other earnings from the previous year
- Previous year's income tax return (IRS Form 1040, 1040A, 1040EZ, Trust Territory tax return, or foreign country tax return)
- Records of untaxed income, such as welfare, Social Security, Aid to Families with Dependent Children (AFDC) or Aid to Dependent Children (ADC), Temporary Assistance to Needy Families (TANF) or veterans benefits
- Current bank statements
- Current mortgage information for businesses and investments
- Business and farm records
- Records of stocks, bonds, and other investments

*Keep these records*! If you file a paper FAFSA, *do not mail* documents from the above list with your form.

(For more information on completing the FAFSA, go to *www.fafsa.ed.gov* and click on *Filling Out a FAFSA*.)

# SFA CLOSE-UPS

## Grants

### Federal Pell Grant

*Type of aid:* Money that does not have to be repaid

*Points of interest:*

- School disburses the funds.
- Amounts are based on full time or half time enrollment status.
- Students receive only one Pell Grant in a school year.
- The Department of Education guarantees participating schools enough money to award Federal Pell Grants to its eligible students.

*Who qualifies?*

The Department of Education uses a standard formula based on the student's Expected Family Contribution.

*How much money could a student receive?*

The allocation varies with the federal budget. The maximum amount for the 2002–2003 school year was $4,000. The award for individual students is calculated on the Expected Family Contribution and the Cost of Attendance.

*How is the money distributed?*

The school can credit the Pell Grant to your school account, pay you directly, or both. Schools must notify students how, when, and how much they will be paid (it's at least once each term).

### Federal Supplemental Educational Opportunity Grant (FSEOG)

*Type of aid:* Money that does not have to be repaid. It goes to students with exceptional financial need.

*Points of interest:*

- There is no guarantee that schools will receive FSEOGs for all eligible students.

- Students who receive Federal Pell Grants are given highest priority.

*Who qualifies?*
Students with the lowest Expected Family Contributions.

*How much money could a student receive?*
The amount varies between $100 and $4,000 a year, depending on when the student applies, the level of need, funds available, and the school's financial aid policies.

*How is the money distributed?*
A school may credit the student's account or pay directly. Payments are made at least once per term.

## Loans

The following three loans—Stafford, PLUS, and Consolidation Loans—are available through two programs: the *Direct Loan Program* (money loaned by the federal government), and the *Federal Family Education Loan (FFEL) Program* (money loaned by private financial institutions such as banks and credit unions). Schools tends to use one or the other program; the major difference is the source of funds. Loan repayment options vary slightly.

Some student loans are partially *subsidized*. This means the Department of Education pays interest while the student is in school and during grace and deferment periods. *Unsubsidized* loans incur interest for the life of the loan.

### Stafford Loans

*Type of aid:* This type of loan is the major educational self-help program.

*Points of interest:*

- A one-time loan fee of up to 4 percent is deducted from the money received by the borrower.
- Interest rates vary annually, depending on prevailing interest rates, but they never exceed 8.25 percent.

*Who qualifies?*

Half-time and full-time students in eligible programs.

*How much money could a student borrow?*

Dependent students may borrow up to $2,625 the first academic year. After completing the first academic year, they may borrow up to $3,500 for the second full academic year. They may then borrow up to $5,500 for each full academic year.

Independent students (and dependent students whose parents are not eligible for Federal PLUS Loans) may borrow up to $6,625 the first academic year, and $7,500 for the second full academic year. They may then borrow up to $10,500 for each full academic year.

*How is the money distributed?*

The school receives the funds, and pays at least two installments. It goes first to tuition and fees, and if applicable, room and board. The student gets the rest.

*When does repayment begin?*

You have a six-month grace period before the first payment comes due. The grace period starts when you graduate, leave school, or drop below half-time enrollment.

*Is it ever possible to postpone or cancel repayment?*

Under certain conditions, you can receive a deferment or forbearance on your loan, which will allow you to temporarily postpone payments. If you apply for a deferment or forbearance, you must continue to make payments until you are notified that the request has been granted, or you could end up in default. In a few circumstances, you can even have your loan discharged (cancelled).

> **TELL ME MORE**
>
> For more information on loan deferments, forbearance, and discharges:
>
> - Through the Direct Loan Program: Contact the Direct Loan Servicing Center at 1-800-848-0979, or visit *www.dlssonline.com*.
> - Through the FFEL Program: Contact your lender or its servicing agent.

## PLUS Loans

*Type of aid:* Money loaned to parents with good credit histories to pay for a dependent child's educational expenses.

*Points of interest:*

- If parents are unable to pass a credit check, they may still be able to receive a PLUS Loan if a relative or friend can pass the credit check and agree to pay in the case that the parents are unable.

- In some instances, parents may pass a credit check if they show legitimate reasons for a poor credit history.
- Parents start the application process by contacting the school's financial aid office.
- Since the PLUS Loan is not based on need, completion of a FAFSA may not be required. School policies vary.
- Interest rates vary annually, depending on prevailing interest rates, but never exceed 9 percent.
- A 4 percent loan fee is deducted proportionately from each payment.

*Who qualifies?*

Parents who meet citizenship requirements as explained in "Who Gets SFA?" earlier in this chapter. They must also be current with payment of other SFA loans in their names.

*How much can parents borrow?*

The annual limit is equal to the Cost of Attendance minus any other financial aid the student receives.

*How is the money distributed?*

The lender sends the money to the school. It is usually paid out in two installments. The funds go first to tuition, fees, other school charges, and room and board if applicable. Any remaining money goes directly to the parents unless they authorize release to the student or to the student's school account.

*When does repayment begin?*

Generally, repayment must begin within 60 days after the final loan disbursement for the period of enrollment for which you borrowed. There is no grace period for these loans. This means that interest begins to accumulate at the time the first disbursement is made. Your parents must begin repaying both principal and interest while you're in school.

## Consolidation Loan

*Type of aid:* A repayment option enabling the borrower to combine several types of federal student loans into one loan with one monthly payment. Even a single loan can be rolled into a Consolidation Loan to take advantage of the flexible repayment options.

*Points of interest:*

- The interest on a Consolidation Loan can be lower than the original loan. Interest rates are fixed for the entire time you are repaying the loan and will never exceed 8.25 percent.
- No money is distributed in Consolidation Loans. They simply enable the borrower to scale down the number of monthly payments.

*Who qualifies?*

Most borrowers may apply for Consolidation Loans. They may apply while still in school or during the repayment period. Schools distribute information about Consolidation Loans during entrance and exit counseling sessions.

## Federal Perkins Loan

*Type of aid:* A low-interest (5 percent) loan. Perkins Loans are not connected with the Direct or Federal Family Education Loan programs.

*Points of interest:*

- Perkins Loans are made from government funds and a share contributed by the school.
- The school is considered the lender on a Perkins Loan.
- Perkins Loans are repaid to the school.
- There are no loan fees.

*Who qualifies?*

The neediest students.

*How much could a borrower receive?*

Depending on the level of need, as well as funds available from the school, a student may borrow up to $4,000 a year.

*How is the money distributed?*

The school usually pays the student directly or credits the school account. Generally, at least two payments are made during the academic year.

*When does repayment begin?*

If you're attending school at least half time, you have a nine-month grace period after you graduate, leave school, or drop below half-time status before you must begin repayment. You may be allowed up to 10 years to repay.

### An Unpaid Creditor Is an Ugly Thing!

When you graduate and those first paychecks roll in, the temptation to spend will seem unbearable. And the grace period will fly by. The monthly loan payments will come due. And you'll have some serious responsibility on your hands.

Financial aid lenders take harsh action when borrowers default (fail to make payments). They notify national credit bureaus, which wrecks your credit rating for a long time. That makes it tough to borrow money for a car or house. Lenders may also deduct payments and collection expenses from your paycheck. The Department of Education could authorize the Internal Revenue Service to deduct the overdue payments from your income tax refunds. Defaulting endangers your chances of receiving more federal financial aid.

Even if you happen not to receive a bill or repayment notice, you're still responsible for paying the set amount. The lender will probably send notices or coupon books in advance, but it's a good idea to watch for them two months before your grace period ends. If nothing arrives, say, six weeks prior to your first payment date, call to be sure everything is in order. Make sure to keep copies of all your loan documents.

If you apply for deferment or forbearance, you're responsible for payments until the lender confirms that your request has been granted. You're responsible for notifying the loan representative if you drop below half-time enrollment, or change your name, address, or Social Security Number.

## Federal Work-Study

*Type of aid:* Jobs to help students pay their educational expenses

*Points of interest:*

- The program encourages community service work and work related to a student's course of study.
- Jobs are both on and off campus. Campus jobs usually involve working for the school.
- Off-campus work-study jobs must be in nonprofit organizations or public agencies. The work must be in the public interest.

*Who qualifies?*

Students with "financial need" as defined by the Department of Education's SFA formulas. The timing of the student's application and available funds determine who receives Work-Study assistance.

*How much money could a student earn?*

Wages are equal to, or higher than, the federal minimum wage, depending on the type of job and skills required. The amount a student earns may not exceed his total Federal Work-Study award. When assigning work hours, the employer or financial aid administrator will consider the student's class schedule and academic progress.

*How is the paycheck distributed?*

The school must pay students directly at least once a month. A student may request deposits to a bank account or application toward school expenses.

> **SEARCH AIDS**
>
> - Keywords to find local groups through the Yellow Pages: *associations, clubs, organizations*
> - Keywords for online searches: *scholarships, grants, financial aid*

## "FREE" MONEY

Scholarships and grants are not just for the academic elite. For sure, some are geared toward academic achievement. But others are based on gender, financial need, field of study, ethnicity, or place of residence—or as incentives to work in a geographic location or line of work. Two- and four-year colleges offer some scholarships and grants. Of course, the tradeoff is the higher cost of attendance than career or technical schools.

We're not going to tell you that free money is easy to come by. You'll have to hustle and sift out the programs for which you qualify. All types of financial aid need to be carefully explored. But we will help you start your search on the right foot.

## Where Do I Start?

A good way to acquaint yourself with the subject is to spend an hour or so browsing through a CD-ROM or a directory of scholarships and grants. If you're in high school, check the resources in the counseling office.

Here's a list of leads for starters. As soon as you get the hang of it, you can delete and add sources specific to your goals.

- State department of education
- City job services agency
- County health department
- Professional societies and associations
- Businesses (some businesses give scholarships to children of employees)
- Labor unions
- Civic groups and fraternal organizations (e.g., American Legion, 4-H Clubs, Girl Scouts, Boy Scouts)
- Charitable and educational foundations
- Religious organizations
- State associations of career educators or career education institutions

## Scholarship Scams

There are many private scholarship search services that provide lists of "sources" of financial assistance you may apply for. If you decide to use one of these services, be sure to check its reputation and track record by contacting the Better Business Bureau or a State Attorney General's Office.

Here are some questionable tactics you should watch out for:

- A service telling you that millions of dollars in student aid go unclaimed every year. The large figures you may hear or read about usually represent an estimated national total of employee benefits or member benefits. Usually, such benefits are available only to the employees (and their families) of a specific company, or to the members of a specific union or other organization.
- A service claiming that you can't get the same information anywhere else. Many services make you pay to get information you could have received for

free from a college financial aid office, state education agency, local library, the U.S. Department of Education, or the Internet. Remember that you can find out about student aid without paying a fee to a search service.

- A service requesting your credit card or bank account number to hold student financial aid for you. Search services do not, in most cases, provide any awards directly to applicants, apply on behalf of applicants, or act as a disbursing agent for financial aid providers. You should never give out a credit card or bank account number unless you know the company or organization you are giving it to is legitimate.

- A service trying to get you to send them money by claiming that you are a finalist in a scholarship contest. Most sources of financial aid have application deadlines and eligibility criteria; they do not, generally, operate like a sweepstakes.

- A scholarship seminar ending with one-on-one meetings in which a salesperson pressures the student to "buy now or lose out on this opportunity." Legitimate services don't use such pressure tactics.

## Good Financial Aid Resources

- *The Student Guide: Financial Aid* is the best federal financial aid overview. It details all the programs discussed in this chapter. It lists websites and phone numbers to related federal and state organizations. Download it or request a free copy from: Federal Student Aid Information Center, P.O. Box 84, Washington, DC 20044-0084. Phone: (800) 433-3243. Website: *www.ed.gov/studentaid*. This website also links you to the Department of Education's vast financial aid services and resources.

- *www.students.gov* is the federal government's huge student website with links to government resources for planning and paying for your education. You can use the site to search for a job, access other government services, and even to file your taxes.

- *Scholarships 2003* (Kaplan, Inc., Simon & Schuster, New York, 2002). This directory features indexes to locate awards for students at various educational levels and fields of study.

- *Directory of Financial Aids for Women 2001–2003: A Listing of Scholarships, Fellowships, Loans, Grants, Awards and Internships* by Gail Ann Schlachter (Reference Service Press, El Dorado Hills, CA, 2001). Assistance is arranged by categories such as scholarships, loans, etc. Programs are also indexed by sponsoring organizations, geographic region in which assistance is granted and subject area. The directory describes 559 programs by application deadline, duration and amount of the award, and eligibility. It lists other directories of assistance for women including books and websites.

- *2000–2002 High School Senior's Guide to Merit and Other No-Need Funding* by Gail Ann Schlachter and R. David Weber (Reference Service Press, El Dorado Hills, CA, 2000). The guide includes state sources of financial aid and grants as well as contests and other awards. Descriptions include the guidelines and deadlines for application. The book also lists websites for additional sources of free money.

- *www.FinAid.org* is a one-stop website for financial aid. It's a free resource for all users and it costs nothing to link to the site. Users may sign up for personalized scholarship leads by keying in data about their educational goals and information related to eligibility for awards. The site explains student loans and offers calculators to figure college costs, financial aid loan payments, and other school-related financial matters.

# Chapter Six

# MOVING AHEAD

Soon after you began to read the Introduction to this book, you came upon this promise: "This little book takes you on a long journey in a short amount of time." You've almost reached the end of the book and the end of this journey. All kinds of possible adventures lie ahead, and you now know more about dozens of them.

- You may have narrowed your choices, or even honed in on a particular career.
- Or, you may simply realize that a degree in business administration is for you because it opens doors that enrich you as you wait to discover precisely what kind of work you'll find most fulfilling.
- You certainly know that you can earn a certificate or an associate's degree, bachelor's degree, or master's degree—and, if you wish, you can earn these without spending time in the traditional classroom, via distance learning.
- You know that a lack of funds isn't a good reason for not getting your degree. Money for an education is out there waiting for you! (And after reading chapter 5, you know where to look for it.)

## EACH CAREER TAKES ITS OWN SHAPE

There are many career paths available for today's business professionals. A *vertical* career path—with a series of jobs progressing up the ladder in one occupation—is one possibility. For example, an associate accountant in an accounting firm will become an accountant, then a senior accountant, then may eventually become a supervisor and perhaps even a partner.

Starting from an entry-level position, your career path could take the following route:

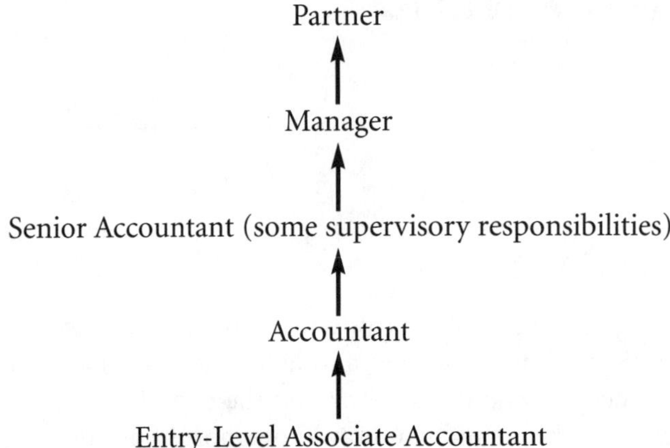


This is only an example, since every business specialty and every company may have a different set of steps to get you to the top.

An alternative career path might be made up of *lateral* moves—similar job responsibilities in different settings. For instance, a public affairs specialist in a governmental agency might be hired to work as a PR specialist in the communications department of a large publishing house. After a few years, she might move to a PR firm, and then eventually decide to work as an independent consultant.

Sometimes, people switch occupations altogether. A loan officer might decide to become a financial planner, for example. He then might switch occupations again, becoming a business teacher or technical writer.

## CLIMBING TO THE TOP OF THE LADDER

How does a person get from college graduate to Chief Executive Officer? Obviously, there's no single formula to follow. Choose an industry that appeals to you—fashion, sports, entertainment, automobiles, (i.e., for profit) or social service or charitable organizations (i.e., not-for-profit)—and groom yourself to grow into the front office!

*Illustration:* John Doe pursues a bachelor's degree in business administration with a concentration in marketing. Doe decides that he should learn everything he can about the advertising business, because the more he knows, the easier it will be to move up the career ladder. That's his goal.

He thinks of his goal during his college years when he works summers in the mail-room at the Brown Advertising Company. He thinks of his goal when he accepts his first "real" job after graduation in the production department of the same company. He is hired at $22,000 a year. His responsibility is to make sure production is timely and deadlines are honored. He doesn't find the work particularly interesting, but he sticks with it to learn all he can. Two years later, he leaves Brown Advertising Company and gets a job as a copywriter in the creative department of Greenlight Ad Agency. He takes a pay-cut and earns $20,000 a year. Now he's writing promotional copy and working with the art director to "brainstorm" in order to design the entire mailing package. He loves the work but struggles to make ends meet. Eight years of this (with some salary increases and promotions) and John quits Greenlight to accept a job in the marketing department of Healthy Heart Frozen Foods.

By this time, Doe is married and has two children. He's earning $60,000 a year as a marketing manager at Healthy Heart. Doe pursues an M.B.A. degree via distance learning in spite of the fact that he travels at least 10 days a month to visit some of the company's 12 global offices. His salary increases again after he earns the M.B.A., and he's promoted to Global Director of Marketing. He also sits on the company's Board of Directors.

John is active in his church and well-liked in this community. It's not unusual to find him raising money to build a new hospital or to upgrade the local park's ball field. He speaks at community functions and his name and photograph are often in the local newspaper to report on some community spirited action he has taken.

By the time John Doe's children enter high school, he is offered and accepts the CEO position at Healthy Heart Frozen Foods. His earnings increase to $400,000 annually.

*Ingredients in the recipe of John Doe's rise to CEO:*

- Willing to work hard
- Willing to try new things and stick to them even when they're not his favorites
- Willing to take less money to accept a position that will add to his skills
- Grooming himself to be a speaker and respected community leader (which reflects well on his company)
- Willing to travel and put in long hours away from home
- Willing to further his education

In short, our John Doe is always alert for ways to fashion himself into the kind of person who is just right for the job—and he is willing to act on his findings.

### CEOs: HOW DID THEY GET TO THE TOP?

**Mike Bowlin, Chairman and CEO, Atlantic Richfield Co. (ARCO)**

Bowlin started in marketing department at R.J. Reynolds. In 1969, he took a job in the human resources department in ARCO's Los Angeles office, then moved to a similar position in ARCO's HR department in Alaska. By 1982, he'd learned enough about the company to move into an executive position in ARCO's oil and gas operations. He continued to rise through the ranks and became chairman and CEO in 1996.

**Jill Barad, CEO, Mattel**

Barad started out as a model and actress in the late 1960s. She took a cosmetology job with Coty Cosmetics and was promoted to an executive position in Coty's marketing department. After taking some time off to get married and have children, she landed a job in Mattel's novelty toy division. By 1985, she'd climbed the ranks to become Marketing Director, and was appointed CEO in 1997.

## YOUR EVOLVING CAREER

Once you start your career in one of the many areas of business administration, you can expect to find your work life changing for several reasons:

- You will need to constantly update your skills to keep up with changes in technology and in your industry.

- You may want to seek new challenges after mastering one area of business.
- You may decide to look for more job security, more interesting work, better pay, or greater decision-making responsibilities.
- You could discover that your calling is toward a specialized niche in your field.
- You might find a better match for your skills in a different occupation.
- You could move into a newly created business occupation.
- You might decide to return to school for an advanced degree or professional certification.

## The Unchanging Core of Your Career

Have you noticed how terms like *expanded*, *layered on*, and *married* are often used in describing career changes? Those words suggest adding on to something that's already in place. And that's exactly what happens—some things stay with you.

No matter how far your career path might take you from your original training and job description, you'll always have that core of inborn skills, traits, and job preferences you identified through the self-assessment tools in the Introduction. If the prospect of an ever-changing work scene shakes you up a bit, you can find security by counting those assets. On the other hand, you may find some exciting challenges when you want to strengthen or tone down any of those skills or traits. Consider those your growth opportunities. You'll find huge satisfaction in your progress.

The knowledge you acquire from your training is another piece of stability. If your career ladder takes you up the ranks of one profession, each new credential or degree will build on the previous one.

Even if your career path doesn't follow a straight vertical line, your existing knowledge and experience will still serve you. Your communication skills will never be out of date, and neither will the work habits that mark you as a star employee.

# CONCLUSION

Opportunities in all areas of business administration are almost limitless for people with initiative and drive. The path begins with self-assessment to analyze which position would best suit you. Then plan a course of study that will lead to those goals you seek. Once you establish a foothold in your career, create opportunities for personal and professional growth by gaining experience in and expanding your knowledge of the product with which you are working and the job you are doing.

All of this means that you can count on two things if you choose a career in business administration: You will find endless opportunities to develop and advance, and you will *never* get bored.

Good luck in your new career!

# DIRECTORY OF RESOURCES

## PROFESSIONAL ORGANIZATIONS

American Accounting Association
5717 Bessie Drive
Sarasota, FL 34233-2399
(941) 921-7747
*http://accounting.rutgers.edu/raw/aaa/*

American Advertising Federation
1101 Vermont Avenue, NW
Suite 500
Washington, DC 20005-6306
(202) 898-0089
*www.aaf.org*

American Association of Advertising Agencies
405 Lexington Avenue
New York, NY 10174
(212) 682-2500
*www.aaaa.org*

American Bankers Association (ABA)
1120 Connecticut Avenue, NW
Washington, DC 20036
1-800-BANKERS
*www.aba.com*

American Finance Association
Haas School of Business
University of California at Berkeley
Berkeley, CA 94729-1900
*www.afajof.org*

American Institute of Certified Public Accountants
1211 Avenue of the Americas
New York, NY 10036
*www.aicpa.org*

American Insurance Association (AIA)
1130 Connecticut Avenue, NW
Suite 1000
Washington, DC 20036
(202) 828-7100
*www.aiadc.org*

American Management Association
1601 Broadway
New York, NY 10019
(212) 586-8100
*www.amanet.org*

American Marketing Association
311 S. Wacker Drive
Suite 5800
Chicago, IL 60606
(800) AMA-1150
*www.ama.org*

American Society for Public Administration
1120 G Street, NW
Suite 700
Washington, DC 20005
*www.aspa.org*

American Society of Association Executives
1575 I Street, NW
Washington, DC 20005-1103
(202) 626-2723
*www.asaenet.org*

Association of Management Consulting Firms
380 Lexington Avenue
Suite 1700
New York, NY 10168
(212) 551-7887
*www.amcf.org*

Business and Professional Women/USA
2012 Massachusetts Avenue, NW
Washington, DC 20036
(202) 293-1100
*www.bpwusa.org*

Chartered Property Casualty Underwriters (CPCU) Society
Kahler Hall
P.O. Box 3009
720 Providence Road
Malvern, PA 19355-0709
1-800-932-2728
*www.cpcusociety.org*

Commercial Finance Association
225 West 34th Street
Suite 1815
New York, NY 10122
(212) 594-3490
*www.cfa.com*

Council of State Governments
2760 Research Park Drive
P.O. Box 11910
Lexington, KY 40578-1910
(859) 244-8000
*www.csg.org*

Direct Marketing Association
1120 Avenue of the Americas
New York, NY 10036-6700
(212) 768-7277
*www.the-dma.org*

Financial Executives International (FEI)
10 Madison Avenue
P.O. Box 1938
Morristown, NJ 07962-1938
(973) 898-4600
*www.fei.org*

Health Insurance Association of America (HIAA)
1201 F Street, NW
Suite 500
Washington, DC 20004-1204
(202) 824-1600
*www.hiaa.org*

Institute for Public Relations
P.O. Box 118400
2096 Weimer Hall
Gainesville, FL 32611-8400
(352) 392-0280
*www.instituteforpr.com*

Institute of Internal Auditors
247 Maitland Avenue
Altamonte Springs, FL32701-4201
(407) 830-7600
*www.theiia.org*

Institute of Management Consultants USA
2025 M Street, NW
Suite 800
Washington, DC 20036-3309
1-800-221-2557
*www.imcusa.org*

International Association of Business Communicators
One Hallidie Plaza
Suite 600
San Francisco, CA 94102-2818
(415) 544-4700
*www.iabc.com*

International Facility Management Association
One E. Greenway Plaza
Suite 1100
Houston, TX 77046-0194
(713) 623-4362
*www.ifma.org*

International Personnel Management Association
1617 Duke Street
Alexandria, VA 22314
(703) 549-7100
*www.ipma-hr.org*

Investment Company Institute
1401 H Street, NW
Washington, DC 20005
*www.ici.org*

National Association of Financial and Estate Planning
525 E. 4500 South
Suite F-100
Salt Lake City, UT 84107
(801) 266-9900
*www.nafep.com*

National Association of Insurance and Financial Advisors
2901 Telestar Court
P.O. Box 12012
Falls Church, VA 22042-1205
(703) 770-8100
*www.naifa.org*

National Association of Insurance Women (NAIW)
P.O. Box 4410
Tulsa, OK 74159
1-800-766-6249
*www.naiw.org*

National Association of Tax Professionals
720 Association Drive
Appleton, WI 54914-1483
1-800-558-3402
*www.natptax.com*

National Black MBA Association, Inc.
180 N. Michigan Avenue
Suite 1400
Chicago, IL 60601
(312) 236-BMBA
*www.nbmbaa.org*

National League of Cities
1301 Pennsylvania Avenue, NW
Suite 550
Washington, DC 20004-1763
(202) 626-3000
*www.nlc.org*

National Management Association
2210 Arbor Boulevard
Dayton, OH 45439
(937) 294-0421
*www.nma1.org*

National Society of Accountants
1010 N. Fairfax Street
Alexandria, VA 22314
1-800-966-6679
*www.nsacct.org*

National Society of Hispanic MBAs
1303 Walnut Hill Lane
Suite 300
Irving, TX 75038
(877) 467-4622
*www.nshmba.org*

Project Management Institute
Four Campus Boulevard
Newtown Square, PA 19073-3299
(610) 356-4600
*www.pmi.org*

Public Affairs Council
2033 K Street, NW
Suite 700
Washington, DC 20006
(202) 872-1790
*www.pac.org*

Public Relations Society of America (PRSA)
33 Irving Place
New York, NY 10003-2376
(212) 460-1466
*www.prsa.org*

Sales & Marketing Executives International, Inc.
P.O. Box 1390
Sumas, WA 98295-1390
(312) 893-0751
*www.smei.org*

Society for Human Resource Management
1800 Duke Street
Alexandria, VA 22314
(703) 548-3440
*www.shrm.org*

Women Executives in Public Relations
FDR Station
P.O. Box 7657
New York, NY 10150-7657
(212) 750-7373
*www.wepr.org*

Women's Institute for Financial Education (WIFE)
P.O. Box 910014
San Diego, CA 92191
(760) 736-1660
*www.wife.org*

## COMPANIES

### Accounting and Finance

Ameritrade Holding Corporation
4211 S. 102nd Street
Omaha, NE 68127
(402) 331-7856
*www.ameritradeholding.com*

American Express
90 Hudson St.
Jersey City, NJ 07302
(212) 640-2000
*www.americanexpress.com*

Charles Schwab
101 Montgomery Street
San Francisco, CA 94104
(415) 627-7000
*www.schwab.com*

Citigroup
153 E. 53rd Street
New York, NY 10043
(212) 559-1000
*www.citigroup.com*

Deloitte & Touche
1633 Broadway
New York, NY 10019
(212) 492-4000
*www.dttus.com*

Deutsche Bank
31 West 52nd Street
New York, NY 10019
(212) 469-5000
*www.db.com*

Dun & Bradstreet
One Diamond Hill Road
Murray Hill, NJ 07974-1218
(908) 665-5000
*www.dnb.com*

Ernst & Young
750 Seventh Avenue
New York, NY 10019
(212) 773-3000
*www.ey.com*

Freddie Mac
8200 Jones Branch Drive
McLean, VA 22102
(703) 903-2000
*www.freddiemac.com*

Goldman Sachs
85 Broad Street
New York, NY 10004
(212) 902-1000
*www.gs.com*

John Hancock Financial Services, Inc.
John Hancock Place
Boston, MA 02117
(617) 572-6000
*www.jhancock.com*

KPMG
345 Park Avenue
New York, NY 10154
(212) 909-5000
*www.kpmg.com*

MasterCard International Inc.
2000 Purchase Street
Purchase, NY 10577-2509
(914) 249-2000
*www.mastercard.com*

MBNA Corporation
1100 N. King Street
Wilmington, DE 19884-0115
(302) 453-9930
*www.mbnainternational.com*

Metropolitan Life Insurance Company
One Madison Avenue
New York, NY 10010-3690
(212) 578-2211
*www.metlife.com*

Morgan Stanley Dean Witter & Co.
1585 Broadway
New York, NY 10036
(212) 761-4000
*www.msdw.com*

PNC Financial Services Group
One PNC Plaza
249 Fifth Avenue
Pittsburgh, PA 15222-2707
(412) 762-1553
*www.pnc.com*

Price Waterhouse Coopers
1177 Avenue of the Americas
New York, NY 10036
(646) 471-4000
*www.pwcglobal.com*

Prudential Financial
751 Broad Street
Newark, NJ 07102-3777
(973) 802-6000
*www.prudential.com*

Sallie Mae
11600 Sallie Mae Drive
Reston, VA 20193
(703) 810-3000
*www.salliemae.com*

State Farm Insurance Companies
One State Farm Plaza
Bloomington, IL 61710-0001
(309) 766-2311
*www.statefarm.com*

Visa International
900 Metro Center Blvd.
Foster City, CA 94404
(650) 432-3200
*www.visa.com*

## Advertising and Public Relations

D'Arcy, Masius, Benton & Bowles
1675 Broadway
New York, NY 10019
(212) 468-3622
*www.dmbb.com*

DDB Worldwide Communications Group Inc
437 Madison Ave.
New York, NY 10022
(212) 415-2000
*www.ddb.com*

Edelman Public Relations
200 E. Randolph Drive
62nd Floor
Chicago, IL 60601
(312) 240-3000
*www.edelman.com*

Grey Global Group
777 Third Avenue
New York, NY 10017
(212) 546-2000
*www.grey.com*

J. Walter Thompson
466 Lexington Avenue
New York, NY 10017
(212) 210-7000
*www.jwtworld.com*

McCann-Erickson WorldGroup
750 Third Avenue
New York, NY 10017
(212) 697-6000
*www.mccann.com*

Ogilvy & Mather
309 West 49th Street
New York, NY 10019
(212) 237-4000
*www.ogilvy.com*

Ruder Finn
301 East 57th Street
New York, NY 10022
(212) 593-6400
*www.ruderfinn.com*

Saatchi & Saatchi
375 Hudson Street
New York, NY 10014
(212) 463-2000
*www.saatchi-saatchi.com*

Waggener Edstrom
Three Stamford Plaza
301 Tresser Blvd.
Suite 1315
Stamford, CT 06901
1-800-938-8136
*www.wagged.com*

Weber Shandwick Worldwide
387 Park Avenue South
New York, NY 10016
(212) 686-6666
*www.shandwick.com*

Young & Rubicam Inc.
285 Madison Avenue
New York, NY 10017-6486
(212) 210-3000
*www.yr.com*

## Miscellaneous

American Greetings
One American Road
Cleveland, OH 44144-2398
(216) 252-7300
*corporate.americangreetings.com*

Borden Foods
180 East Broad Street
Columbus, OH 43215
(614) 225-4000
*www.bordenfamily.com*

Campbell Soup Company
Campbell Place
Camden, NJ 08103-1799
(856) 342-4800
*www.campbellsoup.com*

Coca-Cola Co.
One Coca-Cola Plaza
Atlanta, GA 30301
(404) 676-2121
*www.cocacola.com*

Colgate-Palmolive
300 Park Avenue
New York, NY 10022
(212) 310-2000
*www.colgate.com*

Dole Food Company, Inc.
1 Dole Drive
Westlake Village, CA 91361
(818) 874-4000
*www.dole.com*

Eastman Kodak Company
343 State Street
Rochester, NY 14560-1139
(716) 724-4000
*www.kodak.com*

General Electric
3135 Easton Turnpike
Fairfield, CT 06431-0001
(203) 373-2211
*www.ge.com*

General Mills
One General Mills Blvd.
Minneapolis, MN 55426
(952) 764-2311
*www.generalmills.com*

Gillette
Prudential Tower Building
Boston, MA 02199
(617) 421-7000
*www.gillette.com*

Hallmark Cards, Inc.
2501 McGee Street
Kansas City, MO 64108
(816) 274-5111
*www.hallmark.com*

Hershey Foods Corporation
100 Crystal A Drive
Hershey, PA 17033
(717) 534-6799
*www.hersheys.com*

Johnson & Johnson
One Johnson & Johnson Plaza
New Brunswick, NJ 08933
(732) 524-0400
*www.jnj.com*

Kraft Foods Inc.
3 Lakes Drive
Northfield, IL 60093-2753
(847) 646-2000
*www.kraftfoods.com*

Levi Strauss & Co.
1155 Battery Street
San Francisco, CA 94111
(415) 501-6000
*www.levistrauss.com*

Mattel, Inc.
333 Continental Boulevard
El Segundo, CA 90245-5012
(310) 252-2000
*www.mattel.com*

Motorola, Inc.
1303 E. Algonquin Road
Schaumberg, IL 60196
(847) 576-5000
*www.motorola.com*

Nabisco
7 Campus Drive
Parsippany, NJ 07054
(973) 682-5000
*www.nabisco.com*

Nike, Inc.
One Bowerman Drive
Beaverton, OR 97005-6453
(503) 671-6453
*www.nikebiz.com*

Nintendo
4820 150th Avenue NE
Redmond, WA 98052
(425) 882-2040
*www.nintendo.com*

PepsiCo, Inc.
700 Anderson Hill Road
Purchase, NY 10577-1444
(914) 253-2000
*www.pepsico.com*

Procter & Gamble
One Procter & Gamble Plaza
Cincinnati, OH 45202
(513) 983-1100
*www.pg.com*

Texas Instruments Incorporated
12500 TI Blvd.
Dallas, TX 75243-4136
(972) 995-3773
*www.ti.com*

Xerox Corporation
800 Long Ridge Road
Stamford, CT 06904
(203) 968-3000
*www.xerox.com*

## WEBSITES

### Career Websites

*Careers.yahoo.com*
*www.acinet.org/acinet*
*www.brassring.com*
*www.careerbuilder.com*
*www.careerexplorer.net*
*www.careeropps.com*
*www.eresumewriting.com*
*www.Headhunter.net*
*www.Hotjobs.com*
*www.Monster.com*
*www.resumania.com*
*www.resume-center.com*
*www.7step-resumesampler.com*
*www.UniversityofLife.com*
*www.vault.com*
*www.WetFeet.com*

## Financial Aid

*www.americorps.org*
*www.dlssonline.com*
*www.ed.gov/studentaid*
*www.fafsa.ed.gov*
*www.FinAid.org*
*www.personalbudgeting.com*
*www.students.gov*

## Other Useful Websites

*hbsworkingknowledge.hbs.edu*
*knowledge.wharton.upenn.edu*
*www.adweek.com*
*www.bloomberg.com*
*www.business2.com*
*www.businessdaily.com*
*www.businessfinancemag.com*
*www.businessweek.com*
*www.businesswire.com*
*www.cfo.com*
*www.factiva.com*
*www.forbes.com*
*www.ftbusiness.com*
*www.hispanicbusiness.com*
*www.hoovers.com*
*www.kiplinger.com*
*www.legal.gsa.gov*
*www.marketingtoday.com*
*www.mbastyle.com*
*www.mediastudies.org*
*www.morebusiness.com*
*www.prweek.com*
*www.smartmoney.com*
*www.valuationresources.com*
*www.worldwidelearn.com*

# Kaplan Higher Education

Kaplan Higher Education,

the higher education division of Kaplan, Inc.

(www.questeducation.com), is a leading education and

career training provider that offers diversified, career-oriented,

postsecondary education to more than 18,000 students at

45 campuses located in 13 states.


Kaplan Higher Education offers a variety of bachelor degree,

associate degree, and diploma/certificate programs in fields such as

health care, information technology, business, legal studies,

electronics, design and graphic arts, and various vocational trades.

Its curricula include programs leading to entry-level employment

in ten of the fifteen fastest growing occupations

(measured by percentage growth from 1994 through 2005)

as projected by the U.S. Department of Labor.

**Kaplan Higher Education**

## ARIZONA

**Long Technical College**
13450 N. Black Canyon Hwy.
Suite 104
Phoenix, AZ 85029
(602) 548-1955

**Phoenix Career College**
First American Title Bldg.
111 W. Monroe Avenue, Suite 800
Phoenix, AZ 85003
(602) 252-2171

## CALIFORNIA

**Andon College**
1700 McHenry Village Way, Suite 5
Modesto, CA 95350
(209) 571-8777

**Andon College**
1201 N. El Dorado Street
Stockton, CA 95202
(209) 462-8777

**California College of Technology**
4330 Watt Avenue, Suite 400
Sacramento, CA 95660
(916) 649-8168

**Maric College**
3666 Kearney Villa Road, Suite 100
San Diego, CA 92123
(858) 279-4500

**Maric College**
2030 University Drive
Vista, CA 92083
(760) 630-1555

**Modern Technology College**
6180 Laurel Canyon Blvd., Suite 101
North Hollywood, CA 91606
(818) 763-2563

## COLORADO

**Denver Career College**
8 South Nevada Avenue, Suite 101
Colorado Springs, CO 80903
(719) 444-0190

**Denver Career College**
1401 19th Street
Denver, CO 80202
(303) 295-0550

## IOWA

**Hamilton College**
2302 West First Street
Cedar Falls, IA 50613
(319) 277-0220

**Hamilton College**
3165 Edgewood Parkway, SW
Cedar Rapids, IA 52404
(319) 363-0481

**Hamilton College**
4655 121st Street
Des Moines, IA 50323
(515) 727-2100

**Hamilton College**
100 First Street, NW
Mason City, IA 50401
(641) 423-2530

**Kaplan College**
1801 E. Kimberly Road, Suite 1
Davenport, IA 52807
(563) 355-3500

### MARYLAND

**Hagerstown Business College**
18618 Crestwood Drive
Hagerstown, MD 21742
(301) 739-2670

**TESST College of Technology**
1520 South Caton Avenue
Baltimore, MD 21227
(410) 644-6400

**TESST College of Technology**
4600 Powder Mill Road
Beltsville, MD 20705
(301) 937-8448

**TESST College of Technology**
803 Glen Eagles Court
Towson, MD 21286
(410) 296-5350

### NEBRASKA

**Bauder College**
Phipps Plaza
3500 Peachtree Road, NE
Atlanta, GA 30326
(404) 237-7573

**Lincoln School of Commerce**
1821 K Street
Lincoln, NE 68508
(402) 474-5315


**Nebraska College of Business**
3350 North 90th Street
Omaha, NE 68134
(402) 572-8500


## NEW HAMPSHIRE

**Hesser College**
25 Hall Street, Suite 104
Concord, NH 03301
(603) 225-9200


**Hesser College**
3 Sundial Avenue
Manchester, NH 03103
(603) 668-6660


**Hesser College**
410 Amherst Street
Nashua, NH 03063
(603) 883-0404


**Hesser College**
170 Commerce Way
Portsmouth, NH 03801
(603) 436-5300


**Hesser College**
1A Keewaydin Drive
Salem, NH 03079
(603) 898-3480

## OHIO

**Ohio Institute of Photography and Technology**
2029 Edgefield Road
Dayton, OH 45439
(937) 294-6155

**Technology Education College**
288 S. Hamilton Road
Columbus, OH 43213
(614) 759-7700

## PENNSYLVANIA

**CHI Institute**
Lawrence Park Shopping Center
1991 Sproul Road, Suite 42
Broomall, PA 19008-3516
(610) 353-7630

**CHI Institute**
520 Street Road
Southampton, PA 18966
(215) 357-5100

**ICM School of Business and Medical Careers**
10 Wood Street
Pittsburgh, PA 15222
(412) 261-2647

**Thompson Institute**
2593 Philadelphia Avenue
Chambersburg, PA 17201
(717) 709-9400

**Thompson Institute**
5650 Derry Street
Harrisburg, PA 17201
(717) 564-4112

**Thompson Institute**
3440 Market Street
Philadelphia, PA 19104
(215) 387-1530

## TENNESSEE

**Southeastern Career College**
2416 21st Avenue South, Suite 300
Nashville, TN 37212
(615) 269-9900

## TEXAS

**Career Centers of Texas—El Paso**
8360 Burnham Road, Suite 100
El Paso, TX 79907
(915) 595-1935

**San Antonio College of Medical and Dental Assistants**
3900 North 23rd Street
McAllen, TX 78501
(956) 630-1499

**San Antonio College of Medical and Dental Assistants**
4205 San Pedro Avenue
San Antonio, TX 78212
(210) 733-0777

**Southeastern Career Institute**
5440 Harvest Hill, Suite 200
Dallas, TX 75320
(972) 385-1446

**Texas Careers**
194 Gateway
Beaumont, TX 77701
(409) 833-2722

**Texas Careers**
6410 McPherson
Laredo, TX 78041
(956) 717-5909

**Texas Careers**
1015 Jackson Keller
San Antonio, TX 78213
(210) 308-8584

**VIRGINIA**

**Dominion College**
5372 Fallowater Lane, Suite B
Roanoke, VA 24014
(540) 776-8381

**TESST College of Technology**
6315 Bren Mar Drive
Alexandria, VA 22312
(703) 354-1005